THE OTHER WORLD

by Margaret Hodges

One Little Drum
What's for Lunch, Charley?
A Club Against Keats
Tell It Again: Great Tales from
Around the World (editor)
The Secret in the Woods
The Wave
The Hatching of Joshua Cobb
Constellation (editor)
Sing Out, Charley!
Lady Queen Anne
The Making of Joshua Cobb
The Gorgon's Head
Hopkins of the Mayflower
The Fire Bringer
The Other World

The Other World
Myths of the Celts

RETOLD BY MARGARET HODGES

ILLUSTRATED BY EROS KEITH

Farrar, Straus and Giroux   New York

To my Celtic grandfather
JOHN MOORE

I bring a branch of Evin's apple tree

"The Isles of the Happy"
Translated by Kuno Meyer

Acknowledgments

Among those who have been generous in helping me to choose sources for this collection and to understand more fully the background and the spirit of Celtic myth, I owe special thanks to Eilís Dillon, author and folklorist, Dublin; Sean O'Sullivan, Department of Folklore, University College, Dublin; Ernest Marwick, Kirkwall, Orkney; the Staff of the Advocates Library, Edinburgh; Professor R. Geraint Gruffydd and Professor J. E. Caerwyn Williams, University College of Wales; Frank Hogg, Principal, College of Librarianship, Wales; Gareth Watts, National Library of Wales.

I also thank Carnegie Library of Pittsburgh and the Hillman Library, University of Pittsburgh, for their unfailing courtesy and patience in making available to me their outstanding collection of folklore, especially of Celtic myth.

Margaret Hodges

Acknowledgment is made to the University of Wales Press for their permission to use a story in the *Welsh Fairy Book* by W. Jenkyn Thomas as the basis for a free retelling of the Merlin myth; to Routledge & Kegan Paul, Ltd., for permission to reproduce "To the Sun" and "To the New Moon" from *A Celtic Miscellany*, edited by Kenneth Hurlstone Jackson, © 1951; to John Murray Ltd. for permission to reproduce the "Poem of Finn" from *Gods and Fighting Men* by Lady Gregory; and to Constable Publishers for permission to reproduce nine stanzas from the poem "The Isles of the Happy" from *Selections from Ancient Irish Poetry*, translated by Kuno Meyer.

Contents

Introduction

This is a collection of stories which have come down to us from the myths of the Celts. Western civilization owes much of its splendor to the "fire-touched lips" of these inspired people.

In general, myths, which clearly or in symbols speak of the gods, are part of the great body of literature called folklore, the lore and wisdom of the people, handed down through the telling of stories long before men began to put them into written form. Mythical heroes win no small personal triumphs but represent the eventual victory of life over death itself. In *The Hero with a Thousand Faces*, Joseph Campbell tells us that the hero of myth never turns away from the challenge of the dangerous adventures that lie before him. He accepts the challenge, and when he returns from his quest, or when he dies in one last glorious adventure, he has won not only for himself but for his people the promise of a new and better life.

Myths move people at all times and in all places, since it is a godlike thing to accept danger, trial, pain, and even death, for the sake of others. Indeed, stories once told about the gods later mingled with stories about ancient kings who were never to be forgotten because they had served their people so well. The Irish Cuchulain was once a sun god; King Arthur has the shining qualities of the ancient Celtic god Artaios. Thus, our understanding as we read must be on at least two levels: the myth of the god and the hero tale of the king.

Later still, the hero kings became simple folk-tale heroes, like the Lad of Luck in this collection. In that tale the hero appears not as god or king. He is only a fisherman's son, poor and of lowly birth, but in him are godlike qualities. The humble folk who listened to such a tale knew that they too carried in them something divine and at their best moments could be heroes.

So it is that myth releases in the listener or the reader a sense of strength and of joy that overrides sorrow. Modern writers, too, have expressed the spirit of myth. James Joyce, the great Irish writer, created a poetic myth in which his hero, Stephen Dedalus, says, "Welcome, O life!" Myth always says yes to life, come weal, come woe. Joyce's last work, *Finnegans Wake*, uses strange musical language to bring together the past, the present, and the future of all mankind. It is a language filled with overtones of the mythical Irish hero, Finn—the title can be read as *Finn again awake*. For the hero of myth can never die; from age to age, he will always come again.

The sense of the Other World was very strong in the Celtic people. Mysticism and recognition of the supernatural were woven through their culture. Although the strength of the mythical hero is "as the strength of ten," he also has help from the Other World. In his time of trial, the gods themselves, sometimes shining and glorious, sometimes in odd disguise, come to his aid. It is the Great Father of all, the Celtic "Red Man of All Knowledge," who helps the hero in the final exploit of "Dermot in the Land-under-Wave."

The Celts seemed to see in the beauty of this earth the reflection of an unearthly beauty just over the edge of the world, far away, but not too far to be glimpsed in mists or sunsets, or in the clear but shifting depths of the sea. Visitors from the Other World were always close by. They were often friendly and helpful but could be capricious, mischievous, or even spiteful, like the Greek gods, whom they somewhat resembled, for the Celts were a people who had learned from many other cultures.

Starting from their original homeland in southern Germany, the Celts had moved at various times into Asia Minor, Greece, Italy, and Spain, perhaps even into Egypt. They were tall and fair-haired, but among them were shorter, darker individuals, a heritage from their wanderings in Mediterranean countries. In "The Champion of Ireland," two of the heroes are fair-haired, but the greatest of the champions, Cuchulain, is "a dark youth. . . . His hair is black, his look draws love, his glance shoots fire, and the hero light gleams around him."

Many of the ancient writers spoke of this "Celtic fire." It was a more important trait of the Celts than their fair or dark complexion. Posidonius, a Roman writer, described the burning eloquence of the Celts, their hot temperament, their reckless bravery. They could abandon themselves completely to joy or grief, they were terrible in battle, and would avenge the slightest insult.

Their wanderings finally brought them, along with their gods, to the Islands of the West, the last outposts of the known world, pounded by the mighty waves of the Atlantic Ocean. There the Celtic culture reached its finest flowering and Celtic myths took their most beautiful form.

According to the mythology, men known as the Fomorians first reached the western limits of Ireland at least five thousand years ago. The Celts followed the Fomorians, arriving in three successive migrations. The earliest Celtic migrants to Ireland, perhaps about 2500 B.C., were the Firbolgs, who were said to have come by way of the isles of Greece, and who overcame the Fomorians. Next came the Tuatha De Danann, a highly cultivated people who brought with them many arts and a well-developed mythology. They were later remembered as gods. They conquered the Firbolgs and drove them to take refuge in hill forts and in caves which the Firbolgs dug beneath the hills. Finally, there came the warlike Milesians, bringing a heritage from the Spanish peninsula. The Milesians had no system of writing, but their bards and poets ranked next to their kings. They committed to memory and handed down stories which contained elements of all the peoples who had gone before them.

In Scotland, the Orkneys, and Wales, other branches of the Celtic people were accumulating myths about the same gods and heroes, known there under different names. In that Celtic corner of France known as Brittany, the myths took on Gallic names and Gallic flavor, but the themes remained Celtic.

More elements were still to become part of Celtic mythology. Roman soldiers came to Britain and brought their gods. Then the first missionaries, like St. Patrick, arrived in the Western Isles. Recognizing that the old myths were an integral part of the Celtic character, these canny teachers not only wrote the stories down for the first time but added to them to show how the old gods had been overcome by the Christian faith. The new versions reduced the powerful gods to mere fairies and sprites. When the pagan Vikings invaded Britain, they contributed their own myths to the magic brew. For example, as the distinguished folklorists Dr. Hugh Marwick and Ernest Marwick show, the Norse giants easily became giants of Orkney, Scotland, Ireland, Wales, and the Isle of Man, keeping their ability to throw huge stones and step from island to island when they wanted to travel abroad. All could build great bridges into the sea, the finest being the Giant's Causeway built by the Irish Finn Mac Cool.

In his *Creatures of Orkney Legend and Their Norse Ancestry*, Hugh Marwick has written, "Possibly we can see in these local tales a dim memory of Ymir, out of whose body, according to the Scandinavian myth, Odin and his brothers built the world, making the seas and lakes of his blood, earth of his flesh, and the sky of his skull." The Vikings, however, destroyed most of the earliest Celtic manuscripts. Today we have only fragments of the Celtic myths as they may have been told by primitive story-tellers, though we can often see the many mythical elements that went into the making of some of the stories. But J. R. R. Tolkien, who has loved myth so long and used it so well, reminds us of the warning given by Sir George Dasent, the great translator of Norse myth: "We must be satisfied with the soup that is set before us, and not desire to see the bones of the ox out of which it has been boiled." After all, it does not much matter to us that Cuchulain was once a sun god, or that behind the figure of Arthur there shines the ancient Celtic god Artaios. What matters is that when we know a little of how these stories have developed from their earliest mythical sources, we can understand the luster that is forever a part of them. The well-loved heroes are part of ourselves, but the light is from the Other World.

Pittsburgh, Pennsylvania
October 1972

THE OTHER WORLD

The Swan Children

When the Celtic people came to Ireland, they brought with them the goddess Dana. The children of Dana, or the Tuatha De Danann, had the gift of music, and the sound of it, with its healing power, runs through this story.

Lir was a Danann god and also a king of Armaugh, whose beautiful palace was tenderly remembered by his children. Two transformations take place. The wicked stepmother, changed into a demon of the air, is like Medea of Greek mythology. When the children, changed into swans, are cared for by a hermit, he links them together, two and two, with silver chains. The chains often appear in myths when a transformation takes place from bird guise to human shape.

According to Celtic mythology, the Danann were finally defeated by mortals, the Milesians, and at last the old pagan gods were replaced by the Christian faith. In this story we see how a much older myth was adapted in the Christian era. The oldest known manuscript for "The Swan Children," also called "The Children of Lir," goes back only to 1718 but was certainly copied or retold from earlier manuscripts.

Today when one sees in Ireland a "fort" or "rath" crowned with grass or ancient trees, no light comes from it, no music is heard, and the people say that mortal men, the Danes, built these forts. But Padraic Colum said that the raths were built long ago, not by Danes but by the Danann. The palaces of the fairies are under the raths to this day. Sometimes the lights are still seen and the music is heard by those who have the gift of seeing and hearing.

One day, in the time before the saints came to Ireland, a young man named Ebric walked by the sea that surges about the Islands of the West. There he saw floating on the water four beautiful white swans. He heard them singing a sad and lovely song. Around the white cliffs above the swans, fluttered and flew all the birds of the air, calling and answering each other, as if they too were charmed by the singing of the swans. For the wonder of it was that these swans sang with the soft sweet voices of children.

> Gone are the heroes of the Danann,
> Gone is our father Lir;
> His palace is dark and deserted,
> Alas for the Children of Lir.

When Ebric heard these words, tears filled his eyes and he cried out to the swans, "Who are you who make me weep with the beauty of your singing? You are something more than you seem."

Then the largest and most graceful of the swans came close to the margin of the water and spoke with a voice like music. "I am the daughter of Lir, chief of the Danann. Of all the Fairy Host he was the most glorious, his shape like a fiery flame. Like the moon, like the sun, like a flaming beacon was our father Lir. These three are my brothers, and all of us are long, long, under a cruel enchantment."

As Ebric listened in amazement, she spoke on. "I am called Finala of the Fair Shoulder. My brothers are Conn, Hugh, and Fiachra. When our mother died, our father married again to give us a new mother who would care for us tenderly, for we were the light of his eyes. Oh, the beauty of our father's palace within the circle of the green hill! In it was nothing rough or harsh, no grief, no gloom, no death, only a beauty of freshness, only a perfume of white blossoms on silver branches."

The voice of Conn took up the song. "When our father's palace opened its doors, the light streamed from it and music poured from it like the harp of the forest."

Hugh sang, "There was no place so fair on the face of the earth! There were golden chariots and chariots of silver and bronze. My father had steeds of yellow gold and others of crimson, others again of heaven's own blue. We, his children, had each a white horse and two white hounds."

"We had each a soft bed spread with a broidered coverlet," sang Fiachra. "We drank from golden cups and ate from plates of silver. Where is it now, our father's palace in the Hill of the White Field, in the Land of the Ever Young?"

Then the voice of Finala sang sadly, "Our stepmother was a woman skillful in magic. There came a day when her heart turned against us because of the great love our father bore us. She took us in her chariot to Lough Derryvaragh, the loneliest lake in all Erin, and there she ordered her servants to kill us. But they refused, saying, 'Evil is the deed you command us to do. We will not kill the dear children of Lir.'

"Our stepmother, wild with rage, would have killed us herself but that her woman's nature made her weak to do it. So when we came to the edge of the lake, she made us go into the water to bathe, speaking to us words like honey. And while we swam there, she worked a great magic upon us so that we were turned into swans. We wept and begged her to tell us how long we must remain under this cruel enchantment. Then she repented what she had done, but had not the power to undo it. She could only grant that we should keep our own voices and that there should be no music equal to our singing."

One by one, the three brothers went on with the story.

"For three hundred years we were doomed to live on the quiet waters of Lough Derryvaragh."

"Three hundred years more she doomed us to wear our lives away in the wild Sea of Moyle that lies between Ireland and Scotland."

"And another three hundred years we must live here in the Isles of the Western Sea. After that, we are free to make our home where we will, but our stepmother's curse will not be broken until a prince of the north weds a princess of the south. Nor can we be free of the spell until a man called St. Patrick comes to Ireland and we hear the sound of a silver bell. These were our stepmother's last words, and we do not know their meaning."

Ebric was lost in wonder. "Have you indeed lived for all those hundreds of years?"

"We have," answered the swan who was Finala. "When the servants told our father of our fate, he came to Lough Derryvaragh and begged us to go home with him, for the evil woman was gone from there forever. In her wickedness, her magic had turned against her so that she had become a Demon of the Air and had flown away. But we could not go home. We had the hearts of wild swans and could live only as swans, feeling the water against our bodies and seeing the sun rise in the open air. So our father bade us a long farewell. He called us the flame of his life, his gladness and his treasure, and we spoke to him in a harmony of song, until his heart was at peace.

"Often he came to us in afterdays, and our kinsfolk came. Harpers and musicians came to listen to our singing, for whoever heard us forgot all sorrow and fell into a sweet sleep from which he woke refreshed. But at last the three hundred years were at an end. When we knew the time was come, we spread our wings and flew northeast to the Sea of Moyle. Bitter it was, that sea, far from family and friends, the wind high and cold, the waves running high. The winter pierced us like a spear. Often we were lost from each other. When we saw that we might be separated forever, we set a meeting place at the Rock of the Seals.

"Soon there came a storm. The wind roared out of the north, thunder and lightning crashed above our heads, and waves cold as ice beat upon us. One by one, we flew to the Rock of the Seals, our feathers draggled and broken, crusted with the salt spray. Our feet were frozen to the icy rocks and we could tear them loose only with pain. The briny water stung our wounds. Nothing could ease our suffering or shorten our days. I nestled my brothers against me, Fiachra under my right wing, Conn under my left wing, and Hugh against my heart. So we comforted each other until the second three hundred years had run their course.

"Then gladly we turned away from the bitter-cold Sea of Moyle and spread our wings to the west. We heard the call of the distant Isles, and we came here to the Isle of Glora, where the voice of the purple sea spoke to us day and night and the little birds sang with us in chorus. But every day was as long as a month, each month long as a year, until the time of our doom drew to an end and we might return to our father in the Land of the Ever Young.

"At last we said to each other, 'This is the day. Let us go home now. The years have been long, long, but our father and our kinsfolk wait for us. Our bright-maned horses remember us, our white hounds do not forget us, for the Land of Youth can never die.'

"And we flew eastward until we looked down on the Hill of the White Field. No light, no music streamed from the hill. Below us, all was silent and dark. Our father's palace was gone. Nettles and brambles filled the hollow where it had stood. Was there ever such sorrow as ours? It was plain to our minds that our father no longer lived. We rested that night on the Hill of the White Field, and we sang our sweetest music for our loss, but there were none to hear us, no Fairy Host, no chiefs of the Danann people, no ladies bright, or harpers, or brave young men with horses and hounds.

"In the morning we rose up early and flew away to the west. Since then we have wandered each day over the islands of Connaught, and every night we have returned to the Isle of Glora. Never again will we see the honey-sweet earth of our youth. Such is the fate of the children of Lir."

From this time on, Ebric loved the swan children greatly, and they loved him. It was he who told their story, so that all knew their fate. Because of this, it was forbidden in Ireland to kill a swan.

Now it happened that the blessed Patrick came at last to Ireland, and after him many other saints. One of them, a hermit, came to the very shore where the swan children lived, and there he built a little chapel of stone. When he chanted his service, the swans listened to his singing, but when he rang a little silver bell, they became afraid. Then

Finala said, "Remember, it is through a silver bell that we shall be set free."

So they came closer and closer to listen, and the hermit came out of the chapel and spoke to the swans. They told him their story, and he told them about the faith of St. Patrick. The hermit took the swans to live with him, and he fed them and loved them, so that no sorrow distressed them. He put a bright silver chain between Hugh and Finala and a chain between Conn and Fiachra.

Then it came about that a prince of the north was to marry a princess of the south of Ireland. She had heard of the wonderful swans, and nothing would do but she must have them for a wedding gift. When the prince sent his men to take the swans, the hermit refused to let them go, and the prince saw that he himself must go to the chapel. There he found the hermit chanting his service, while the swans responded with sweet voices.

When Finala saw the prince, she said to her brothers, "Do not be afraid. The time of our release is near." And as the prince took hold of the swans, two in each hand, their feathers turned into soft white garments, and the children of Lir stood before him, more ancient than the

oldest of God's creatures. The prince of the north fled trembling from that place.

But the children of Lir gathered about the hermit with joyful faces. "Baptize us quickly, for the love you bear us," said Finala, "but do not grieve for us, for we shall never die. We shall return to the Land of the Ever Young. Lay us in one grave. Let Conn be on my left side, Fiachra on my right, and let Hugh rest against my heart. As we were in the days of our sorrow, so let us be forever."

The good hermit baptized the swan children and bowed his head in prayer. When he raised his eyes, the bodies of the children of Lir were dust, but above him their spirits sang, young and beautiful, raising their hands in farewell. Their faces shone and they were clothed in radiance as if great doors were opened for them and light streamed upon them from the Land of Youth.

The Champion of Ireland

Cuchulain (pronounced Coo-hoo-lin) was part god, part epic hero. His father Lugh (pronounced Loo) was the sun god, the Celtic Apollo, and Cuchulain himself, like the sun, had by choice a short and brilliant life. He was so strong that he broke seventeen sets of weapons before he was given some that could withstand his blows. The hero light shone around him in battle and his hero leap could take him over all obstacles. The Celtic warriors who rushed to battle naked and with total disregard for their own safety were true followers of Cuchulain.

In this story Cuchulain appears at the court of Conor (or Conchobhar), who was king of Ulster, one of the Irish kingdoms, about the first century A.D.

Bricriu, the mischiefmaker, is a Celtic counterpart of the Scandinavian Loki. Curoi, the wizard, is a mysterious character who, in other stories, acts as a guide to the Other World and brings the changes of day and night.

The final test which decides the Championship of Ireland is the same as that in the Arthurian story of Sir Gawain and the Green Knight.

"The Champion of Ireland" is one of many stories in the Ulster heroic cycle, told as early as the first century A.D. and retold over hundreds of years until they were written down in the tenth or eleventh century in the monastery of Clonmacnoise on the river Shannon. Early manuscripts telling the story of Cuchulain still exist and can be found in Dublin and in London at the British Museum.

Cuchulain was the nephew of King Conor of Ulster, and his father was no mortal man but the great god Lugh, a name which means Light. Cuchulain, being half god, was no ordinary boy. At King Conor's court in Armaugh, where he grew up, he beat all the other boys in games before he was five years old.

The day Cuchulain was seven, he heard a wise Druid say to the older boys, "If you take arms today, your name will be great in Ireland but your life will be short." That very day, Cuchulain asked his uncle for a sword and armor.

By the time he was seventeen, he had no peer among the champions of Ulster, or indeed of all Ireland. If need be, he could leap over the highest wall, and in battle a hero light, bright as the sun, shone from him. The men of Ulster searched throughout Erin to find a bride fit for so great a champion, but Cuchulain went wooing for himself and chose Emer, the most lovely and virtuous maiden to be found in the country. Emer loved Cuchulain at first sight, but she would not wed him until he had proved his worthiness and constancy. At the end of a year she became his bride, and they lived at Armaugh. There, at the court of King Conor, Cuchulain was one of the heroes of the Red Branch, the king's bodyguard.

Now it happened that one of the chiefs, Bricriu of the Bitter Tongue, was a mischiefmaker. Bricriu invited all the heroes to his dwelling for a feast, planning to stir up strife. He went first to the mighty Leoghaire and said, "All good be with you, Winner of Battles! Follow my advice and you shall be Champion of Ireland forever."

"What is your counsel?" asked Leoghaire.

"When the feast begins," said Bricriu, "bid your chariot driver to claim for you the Champion's Portion of the meat."

"I will do it," answered Leoghaire.

Bricriu next met Conall Cearnach, another chief of the Red Branch, and said to him, "May all good be with you, our Defense and Shield. Bid your chariot driver to claim for you the Champion's Portion of the best meat at the feast, and you can be Champion of Ireland." Bricriu continued his flattery until he had roused up the ambition of Conall Cearnach.

Then Bricriu met the young hero Cuchulain. "May all good be with you, Cuchulain," he said. "You are our joy and our darling, the Hero of Ulster. You can be Champion of Ireland if you order your chariot driver to claim for you the Champion's Portion of the tenderest meat at the feast."

"By the great god Lugh, I shall have it," answered Cuchulain.

When King Conor and his court had entered the house of Bricriu and sat down at the feast, the mischiefmaker cried, "Let the Champion's Portion be given to the best hero in Ulster."

The meat was carved and the three chariot drivers leaped to their feet, each claiming the Champion's Portion for his master. A great fight began. At last King Conor said, "Put up your swords before any man is wounded. The Champion's Portion at this feast shall be divided among the three—Leoghaire, Conall, and Cuchulain. But the king and queen of Connaught shall say who is the greatest champion. All three heroes must go to Connaught for the judgment." This plan pleased everyone but Bricriu.

When the feast was ended, the women rose to leave the table. Bricriu hurried after them into the courtyard, where he caught up with the wife of Leoghaire. "Truly, in beauty and birth, no woman in Ulster is your equal," said he. "If you enter the hall first tonight, you will be queen of the women of Ulster." And so he said to Conall's wife also.

When Bricriu caught up with Emer, the wife of Cuchulain, he said, "Health be with you, Emer, wife of the best man in Ireland! As the sun outshines the stars, so do you outshine all other women. Enter the hall first tonight, for whoever does so will be queen of all the women in Ulster."

The three beautiful women watched one another carefully, and when one went toward the house, the others went with her, step for step, until all three came running like the wind itself. But Emer outran the others and would have entered the hall first, except that the door was shut and bolted. Then followed bitter complaints from the other two, until King Conor let them come in and promised them that their heroes should have a fair judgment by the king and queen of Connaught.

Leoghaire and Conall had their chariots made ready at once and started for Connaught. But Cuchulain stayed on at Armaugh because he took great pleasure in Emer's company. His chariot driver reproached him for lagging behind, saying, "Will you lose the Championship through laziness? The others are far, far ahead."

But Cuchulain answered, "There is still time. Yoke my steeds to the chariot."

Now Cuchulain had two magic horses, the Gray of Macha and the Black Sainglain. When they were yoked to the chariot, he soon came up with the other two heroes, and all three drove furiously on to Connaught.

As they came near, the queen's fair daughter, princess of Connaught, looked from her window and cried, "Mother, I see chariots coming."

"Who comes first?" asked the queen.

"I see a big stout man with reddish-gold hair and long forked beard. He is dressed in purple with gold adornments, and his shield is bronze, edged with gold. He bears a javelin in his hand."

"I know him well," said the mother. "He is Leoghaire, the Storm of War, the Knife of Victory."

"I see another chariot bearing a fair man with long wavy hair. He wears a white robe and a cloak of blue and crimson. His shield is brown, with a bronze edge."

"That is Conall the Victorious."

"Yet a third chariot comes," said the princess. "In it stands a dark youth, most handsome of all the men of Erin. He wears a crimson tunic, brooched with gold, and over it a long white linen cloak. His hair is black, his look draws love, his glance shoots fire, and the hero light gleams around him. His shield is crimson, with a silver rim, and images of beasts shine on it, worked in gold."

"That is the hero Cuchulain," said the queen. "He is the most to be feared by his foes."

"The men of Ulster follow," said the princess. "The earth quakes beneath their chariots and their sound is like thunder or the dashing waves of the sea."

When the king of Connaught heard what had brought the heroes to his hall, he feasted them for three days. Then, needing help to test the three, he went to the Fairy People of the Hills, who said they would willingly aid him. That night they sent three magic and monstrous cats into the room where the heroes were sleeping.

Leoghaire and Conall woke in a fright, clambered up among the rafters, and stayed there all night. But Cuchulain waited until one of the cats attacked him, and then struck a mighty blow. At once, the cats drew back and cowered in a corner. Cuchulain kept watch until daybreak, when the cats disappeared. King Conor came in the morning and laughed to hear how Leoghaire and Conall had spent the night.

"Are you willing now to yield the Championship to Cuchulain?" he asked.

But they answered, "Indeed, no. We are used to fighting men, not monsters."

Now the queen of Connaught began to dread the wrath of Leoghaire and Conall if Cuchulain was judged the Champion, so she thought of a way to be rid of all three. Secretly she called Leoghaire to the king's room and said, "Welcome, greatest of the warriors of Ulster! To you we give the Championship, and in token we give you this cup of bronze with a silver bird embossed on it. Show it to no man until you return to King Conor in the Red Branch House at Armaugh."

To Conall she gave a silver cup with a bird embossed in gold, but to Cuchulain a golden cup with a bird designed in precious gems. The heroes, well content, rode back to Armaugh, each carrying his cup covered and hidden in a fair cloth.

That evening at King Conor's court when the Champion's Portion was carved, Leoghaire rose to claim it, showing his bronze cup. Then Conall the Victorious uncovered his silver cup. But before either could take the Champion's Portion, Cuchulain brought forth his golden cup, and the dispute began all over again.

"If the king and queen of Connaught could not decide

who is Champion, you must go to Curoi the wizard," said King Conor. "Curoi will decide." And to this they all agreed.

The next day the three heroes rode to Kerry, where Curoi dwelt in a hill fort by the sea. Curoi had gone away to plan magic tests for the heroes, whose coming he expected. But the wizard's wife greeted them and asked Leoghaire to spend the night outside the walls, guarding the fortress. Then she worked a charm which sealed all the gates after nightfall, and Leoghaire thought that he would have an easy task.

But late at night a great shadow arose from the sea. The shadow came closer, and Leoghaire saw that it was a huge giant carrying spears made of mighty oak trees. He hurled his spears at Leoghaire, then took him up, squeezed the breath from his body, and hurled him, half dead, over the magic walls of the fort. By morning, Leoghaire had come to himself, and all the men thought that he had leaped over the wall. Leoghaire kept silence and let them believe it. Only Curoi's wife knew the truth.

On the second night Conall took the watch and fared exactly as Leoghaire had. Nor did he confess that the giant had flung him over the wall, and he too won great praise for having made such a mighty leap. But Curoi's wife was silent.

The third night was Cuchulain's turn. About midnight he saw nine gray shadowy forms creeping toward him from the sea. "Who goes there?" he cried. "If you be friends, stop; if foes, come on!"

With that, the shadows raised a shout and fell upon him, but he fought them back and slew them, one and all. A second and a third time came ghostly foes from the sea, but Cuchulain slew them all. Then, wearied out, he sat down to rest.

While Cuchulain sat there, he heard a sound like the surge of waves and beheld a monstrous dragon rising from the water. It came toward him, devouring everything in its way. When the dragon saw Cuchulain, it rose into the air, then flew swiftly down with frightful jaws spread wide. Cuchulain sprang up and his strength came upon him again. Then, giving his hero leap, he thrust his arm down the dragon's throat, found its heart, and tore it out. The monster fell dead on the ground.

Toward daybreak came a great shadow from the sea, and Cuchulain saw the giant with spears made of oak trees. "This is a bad night," roared the giant.

"It will be worse yet for you," said Cuchulain.

The giant, as he had done before, threw his oak-tree spears, but missed Cuchulain. When he tried to grapple with the hero, Cuchulain drew his sword. In his anger, the hero light shone around him and he leaped high enough to give the giant a stroke that brought him to his knees. "Life for life, Cuchulain," said the giant, and vanished.

Now Cuchulain was very tired. He would gladly have leaped into the fort to rest as he thought his comrades had done. Twice he tried to leap the high wall, and twice he failed. Then in his wrath, his great strength came upon him, and the hero light shone around him. He took a little run, leaning on his spear, and leaped so high and so far that he came down in the middle of the fort. Curoi's wife saw him, and heard him sigh. "That is not the sigh of a beaten man," she said. "It is the sigh of a weary conqueror." Cuchulain lay down to rest.

The next morning Curoi's wife said to Leoghaire and Conall, "I know what Cuchulain has endured in the past night. Surely you see now that you are not equal to him."

But they answered, "Cuchulain's friends from the Fairy People of the Hills came to conquer us. The fight was not fair."

"All three of you must go home then to Armaugh," said the wizard's wife. "Wait there until Curoi himself brings his decision." So they bade her farewell and went back to the Red Branch House in Armaugh with the dispute still unsettled.

Curoi gave no sign of coming, but sometime after this, when all the heroes were in their places except Conall and Cuchulain, a terrible Stranger walked into the hall of King Conor. The Stranger was huge and hideous, with wild yellow eyes. He wore the skin of a beast, and over that a gray cloak. In one hand he held a great tree torn up by the roots, and in the other an ax. This giant strode up the hall and leaned against a carved pillar beside the fire.

"Who are you?" asked bold King Conor. "You stand there like a candlestick. Did you come to light our house, or to burn it down?"

"I would do neither," said the Stranger. "My name is Uath, and I seek that which I have never found in the whole world. I seek a man who will keep a certain promise."

"What is the promise?" asked King Conor.

"Behold my ax," said Uath. "The man who will cut off my head today with this ax must let me cut off his head tomorrow. If you have no such champion, I will say that

Ulster has lost her courage and honor."

Leoghaire laughed to himself. "By my word," he said, "I am that champion. Stoop down, fellow, and let me cut off your head. You may take mine tomorrow."

Uath chanted magic spells over the ax and stroked the edge. He laid his head on a block, and Leoghaire smote such a blow that the ax severed the head from the body. Then the body of Uath rose, took up the head and the ax, strode away down the hall, and passed into the night. Leoghaire put on a bold face, but he was afraid.

When the next evening came, in strode Uath the Stranger, as well and sound as before. In his hand he carried the ax. He looked around the hall for Leoghaire, but Leoghaire was not to be seen among the heroes of the Red Branch. His heart had failed him. And the Stranger jeered at the men of Ulster because Leoghaire dared not take a blow as well as give one.

Conall the Victorious was in his place that night and he rose up and made the same agreement with Uath. The Stranger put his head on the block and Conall beheaded him. But again Uath walked out carrying his head, and again when he returned the following evening, the champion was not to be found. Conall would not face the blow.

Uath taunted them all. "Is there not one man of courage among you Ulstermen? Where is that youth Cuchulain? A poor fellow he is, but I would like to see if his word is better than the word of your other heroes."

"A youth I may be," said Cuchulain, "but I will keep my word." Thereupon he leaped up, caught the deadly ax, and severed the giant's head as he stood. But Uath the Stranger walked out with his head, as before.

The next day Cuchulain sat sorrowfully in his place, waiting for certain death. He regretted his rash promise, but he had no thought of breaking his word. Toward the end of day, Uath strode into the hall and stood with the great ax ready.

"Where is Cuchulain?" he cried.

And Cuchulain answered, "Here I am."

"Ah, poor boy," said Uath, "the fear of death lies heavy on you, but you have kept your promise."

Cuchulain rose from his seat and went toward Uath. He knelt, stretched out his neck, and laid his head on the block to receive the blow. Uath raised his ax and brought it down with a crash that shook the house. All men looked fearfully at Cuchulain. But the ax had not touched him. He knelt there unharmed, and leaning on the ax was no terrible Stranger but Curoi, the wizard of Kerry, come to give his decision at last.

"Rise up, Cuchulain," said Curoi. "There is none among all the heroes of Ulster to equal you in courage and loyalty and truth. The Championship of Ireland is yours, the Champion's Portion at all feasts is yours, and your wife shall have the first place among all the women of Ulster."

Then the Red Branch heroes gathered around Cuchulain, acclaiming him Champion of Ireland. And so he is called to this day.

How Finn Mac Cool
Got His Wisdom Tooth

It is supposed that Finn Mac Cool lived in the south of Ireland and fought for the High King at Tara about the third century A.D. Finn's men and other roving bands of warriors were called the Fianna. Stories about him are rooted in much older myths and range freely all over the Celtic lands of the British Isles and into the world of magic. In Scotland he was known as Fingal and he was well known on the Isle of Man. On the Isle of Skye there is a high rock formation called the Wall of the Fianna, and a mountain known as Fingal's Seat. Felix Mendelssohn was inspired to write an overture about Fingal's Cave on the little island of Staffa.

One of the mythical tales about Finn concerned a magic well. There swam in it a heavenly Salmon who ate hazelnuts filled with wisdom from trees of the Other World. Not even the gods were allowed to eat the hazelnuts, but Boann, wife of the Dagda who was chief of the Danann, ate one of them. At this, the waters of the well rose up to drown her and she ran away. The water followed her and became the river Boyne with the Salmon of Knowledge still swimming in it.

The Fianna loved hunting even better than fighting, but later stories show them protecting Ireland against the Norsemen. The Fianna also displayed their godlike strength by fighting against the supernatural powers of darkness which attacked their country or came against the High King at Tara. Indeed, Finn, with his shining fair hair, may be another name for Lugh, the bright sun god. In Celtic mythology, both fight against fiery monsters, as Finn does in this story.

Yet Finn's son Oisin (or Ossian) knew St. Patrick. Once again, we are reading stories which reach back to a time before written history and span the ages until the dawn of Christianity.

After Cuchulain, there came another hero to Ireland, and he was called Finn Mac Cool, a name that means "the fair-haired son of Cool." Finn was the son of Cool Mac Trenmor, chief of the Fianna, a brave band of warriors who served the High King at Tara.

Finn knew that his mother was the fairest lady in all Ireland, and he loved her well, but he had never seen his father, for rival clans were forever fighting each other, and soon after his marriage, Cool Mac Trenmor led the Fianna into battle. In that battle Cool died, killed by Lia, a man of Clann Morna. Lia took from Cool's body his weapons of honor, the spearhead, helmet, shield, and gold-clasped belt which marked him as chief of the Fianna. Lia put these things into a certain precious Treasure Wallet, made of crane skin, dyed scarlet and blue, and rode away from the battlefield.

After Cool's death, Goll Mac Morna, the one-eyed, became leader of the Fianna. But Cool's best men, mourning for their lost leader and for the stolen weapons of honor, fled westward into the wild forests and heathery hills, where they hid among the thickets in huts woven of branches.

Shortly thereafter, a son was born to Cool's beautiful widow. Now it had been prophesied that the old king, her father, would lose his kingdom because of his grandson. So, no sooner was the child born than the wicked old man threw him out of the castle window into the loch below, and went off, satisfied that he was rid of the baby. But the boy did not stay under water. Before long, he came to the surface, brought there by a live salmon he held in his hand.

It happened that Cool's old mother, a Wise Woman, was standing by the loch, a brindled hound by her side. When she saw what happened, she said, "I will save the life of my dead son's child." She waded into the water, seized the child, and rushed off into the forest before anyone could stop her, the hound running beside her.

Deep in the forest the Wise Woman found a great oak tree into which she cut a hole the size of a small room. As she hollowed out the trunk of the oak tree, the wood chippings fell as fine as bran and the hound ate them.

"You'll be called Bran from this day on," she said. Bran was a hound of magic power.

For five years the old grandmother kept Finn and the hound Bran in the hollow of the oak tree. Then she said to Finn, "Come out and I will teach you to walk." When he had learned to walk, she cut a hawthorn switch and said, "Run around the oak tree and I will run after you with the switch. I will strike you as often as I can. Then you shall follow me with the switch and strike me as often as you can."

The first time they ran around the tree, Finn's grandmother struck him many times, and when he chased her he could not strike her at all. But every time they ran, she struck him less and less and he struck her more, until after three days she could not strike him once and he struck her at every step.

"Now I will teach you to leap," said the old woman. She dug a pit at the foot of a high wall and made Finn jump out. Each time he jumped out, she dug the pit deeper. At last she dug the pit so deep that Finn stood in it up to his shoulders. But up he jumped, out of the hole and over the wall with one leap.

When Finn was fifteen years old, his grandmother gave him a spear that she had taken from the Fairy Folk. It was wrapped in a crimson cloak so fine that it could pass through a finger ring and so strong that nothing could pass through it. Finn felt the spear trembling within the cloak as if it longed to be free. Then Finn's grandmother went with him to a hurling match between the forces of his wicked old grandfather and those of another king. Neither side could win until Finn entered the game, playing on the side against his grandfather. Finn won every game. When the old king saw that the fair-haired young hero had won, he was very angry and shouted, "Who is that *fin cumbal*, that towhead?"

"It is a good name for him," said the old woman. "*Fin cumbal* he is and Finn Mac Cool he shall be."

When the old king heard that, he ordered his men to catch Finn and put him to death, but Finn and his grandmother ran off with Bran beside them, a hill at every leap, a glen at every step, and the horses of the old king coming hot behind them. When Finn grew tired, the old grandmother took him on her back and put his two feet in the pockets of her dress, one on each side. Then she ran on as fast as ever, a hill at every leap, a glen at every step.

After a time she said to Finn, "What do you see behind us?"

"I see a rider on a white horse," said Finn.

"Never mind," said she. "A white horse cannot stay the course."

On they sped, until the old woman spoke again. "I feel something coming behind. Look back and see what is it."

"It is a man in armor riding a brown horse," said Finn.

"Never mind that," said his grandmother. "No brown horse can overtake us." On she rushed like the wind, a hill at every leap, a glen at every step, until a third time she felt something coming. "Look around, Finn. What is it?"

"I see a warrior on a black horse following fast, and after him come all the king's men."

"There is no escape this time," said she. "No one can outrun or outlast a black horse. I have had my life. Now one or both of us must die, so I will save you, for you must live to be the chief of the Fianna. I would sooner get my own death by the fox than let my nestling be killed by him. Jump down from my back, take the hound with you, and run as fast as you can. In the path of the black horse is a bottomless bog. I will jump into it and keep afloat up to my neck. When the man comes on his black horse, I will tell him you are in the bog. Now go, and make your old grandmother proud of you."

Finn knew that there was nothing for it but to obey her as he had always done, so down he jumped and away he ran with Bran at his side. The old woman came to the bog, leaped in, and sank up to her neck. When the man on the black horse came, followed by all the king's men, they saw her there and called out, "Where is Finn?"

"He is here in the bog," said she. "Come and help me find him." Then all the king's men leaped into the bog and sank so deep they never came up.

Finn and Bran ran on until they were out of danger. When they came to the Boyne, they saw a place where the river widened into a pool and the silvery water swirled and circled and rose in a rainbow mist. Beyond the pool, with a voice like music from the heart of the earth, the river plunged into a deep cavern and disappeared underground.

Finn saw hundreds of trout and salmon swimming and leaping in the sparkling pool. On the bank stood a man dressed like a fisherman, a casting net in his hand. He caught many crimson-spotted trout, but he threw them all back. When Finn saw this he said, "You must be a hard man to please."

"I am not looking for any ordinary fish," said the man. "I am after catching the Salmon of Knowledge."

"My grandmother told me about that Salmon," said Finn. "It swims in the heavenly waters of the Other World and no mortal man can catch it or even see it."

"That is true," said the man, "but all things in the Other World have their shadows in this world, and though the Salmon of Knowledge be but the shadow of the heavenly Salmon, it is written that a poet of my name shall catch it here. I am Finnegas and I am a poet."

"Then I will stay and serve you," said Finn. And so he did, for he saw that the poet could think of nothing but the Salmon of Knowledge. Finn brought to Finnegas watercress from the river's edge and herbs from the forest. He became the finest woodsman in all Ireland. He learned the name of every blossom and bird. He knew the cackling of ducks, the chattering of the blackbirds, the whistle of the eagle. With sling and snare he caught wild game and cooked it over an open fire as his grandmother had taught him to do. In return, Finnegas taught Finn the art of poetry

and the ancient tales of his people, until Finn himself won the poet's praise for his verses.

There came a day when Finn returned from hunting and saw on the river bank a speckled salmon with scales of silver. Above the melody of the waters he heard a shout of triumph from the poet. "I have him! I have caught the Salmon of Knowledge!"

"I will broil it for you," said Finn, "and may you eat it with good appetite." He built a fire and began to broil the salmon. But as it cooked, a blister formed on one side. Finn pressed the blister, burned his thumb, and put it in his mouth to ease the sting. The tip of his thumb touched one of his teeth and a small fish scale touched his tongue. Immediately a strange feeling shot through Finn as if he knew everything that was happening in all Ireland, and everything that would happen in the future.

When the salmon was nicely cooked, he carried it to Finnegas, but the poet, looking into Finn's face, said, "Something has happened to you. Did you eat of my salmon?"

"No," said Finn. "I only touched the salmon, but when I touched it, I burned my thumb and put my thumb into my mouth. That is all."

"It is enough," said the poet. "Now it is you, not I, who have the wisdom of the Salmon of Knowledge. I do not understand it. The prophecy said that a poet named Finnegas or Finn would eat the Salmon of Knowledge, and I am Finnegas."

The other said, "I am called Finn, and you have made me a poet."

"So the prophecy was meant for you," said Finnegas. "I must be content. I am old, I have had my day. You are young and full of life. Now eat all of the Salmon and go your way."

"I will not part from you forever," said Finn. "When I am chief of the Fianna, like my father before me, I will bring you to my court and we will make poetry the art of heroes." Then he ate the rest of the Salmon, said farewell, and went on his way with Bran beside him, to look for his father's old warriors among the wild hills of the west.

From that time on, whenever Finn needed wisdom, he had only to bite his thumb. At once he knew about far-off events and he knew what he should do. He had great power as a hunter and warrior, as a poet and seer, so that a band of bold young heroes soon gathered around him and followed as he led the way to Connaught, searching for the oldest and best men of the Fianna.

Finn and his men had no sooner crossed the border into Connaught than they came upon a poor woman weeping at the side of the road by the body of her dead son. Her grief touched Finn's heart.

"Who has done this thing?" he asked.

"Lia of Clann Morna has killed my son," said the woman, "and I have no man to avenge his death."

"I will avenge it," said Finn, and he sped along the road until he overtook Lia of Clann Morna and destroyed him entirely. When Lia lay dead, Finn saw that he had at his belt a curious wallet made of crane skin, dyed blue and scarlet. He opened the wallet and found in it a helmet and shield, a spearhead and a belt with a clasp of gold. They seemed like good things to have, so Finn tied the wallet to his own belt and went on with his men and with Bran beside him. Suddenly Bran ran ahead, barking joyfully. Finn and his comrades followed until they came to a clearing in the forest. Around the clearing were huts made of branches and wattles, daubed with mud. At the sound of Bran's barking, old men came from the hovels, each one with a sword or a spear in his hand, thinking that an enemy was attacking. They were thin and bent and tattered, but they were ready to die fighting if need be. Finn knew them at once for his father's men, the heroes of the Fianna. He knelt before them, and having no other gift to give, he held out the wallet.

The old men looked at it. They looked at Bran. Then the oldest said to Finn, "Who are you who come here with the Hound and the Treasure Wallet of the Fianna?"

Finn said, "I am the son of Cool Mac Trenmor, though I never saw my father. My grandmother gave me this hound and I took the wallet from the body of a man named Lia of Clann Morna, whom I killed in fair fight."

"Then you have brought back our honor," said the oldest of the Fianna. "Lia of Clann Morna killed your father."

"I have come to take my father's place if you will have me as your chief," said Finn. "It is now harvest time and the feast of Samhain, when all chiefs and warriors meet together with the High King at Tara, as they did in the old days. I will lead you there as my father did before me."

But the old men answered, "You have young men to follow you now to Tara. We are too old to go. Only leave us the Treasure Wallet of the Fianna as a token of our honor. We will keep it for you until you come again."

So Finn bade farewell to his father's men and went on with his comrades until he came to a hilltop where he looked down on Tara. Its walls and towers shone white in the sunlight and silken banners streamed from its gold-thatched roofs. North, east, south, and west, all roads to Tara were crowded with chiefs in chariots of bronze and silver and with warriors on foot. Finn and his men joined the throng and passed through the great gate. They went into the hall of the High King, where Conn of the Hundred Battles, who ruled at Tara, sat in his seat of state.

Finn sat down near the seat of state where he could both see and be seen. Wrapped in its crimson cloak, the Spear of Power quivered in his hand, and Bran lay down at his side. The harp sounded and a thousand candles shone bright, but the heroes of Tara took no joy in the harvest feast. They spoke of only one thing. For nine years, at Samhain tide, a monster had come to Tara by night, breathing fire and setting the palace aflame. He was known by the name of Allyn. No warrior could kill him, for he came out of the Mountain of Cullion, the home of the great god Manannan, and with him came fairy music that put to sleep every man who heard it. It was said that the monster came to Tara because of a spear, taken long ago from the Fairy People, but where the spear was, no one knew.

Tonight the monster would come again and the king had offered a great reward. Any hero who could destroy Allyn might have his heart's desire, be it a capful of gold, the best of the king's horses, or the fairest of all the women at Tara. Finn listened and bit his thumb. Then he spoke out in a voice that silenced the hall.

"King of Ireland, if I protect Tara from the flames this night, will you give me my wish?"

"You shall have it indeed," said the king. "But who are you and what is your lineage?"

"I am Finn Mac Cool, and I want the leadership of the Fianna, like my father before me."

"You shall have that, if you destroy Allyn," said the king. Once again the company of voices rose in the hall and the harp sounded. But Goll Mac Morna, who had led the Fianna since the death of Cool, sat silent and frowning. His one eye glared at Finn Mac Cool.

About midnight, when the harpist was weary and the candles burned low, there came to the listeners a new sound, music as soft as the wind that blows over the bogs and as sweet as silver bells on a golden bough. One by one, the heroes of Tara fell asleep. Even Bran slept, his head on his paws.

But Finn Mac Cool went from the hall with his spear in his hand and looked out over the ramparts. Now the music was all around him, weaving a spell, faint as a whisper, the fairy music that brings sleep. Finn longed for sleep. His eyelids were heavy with sleep, but he dared not close them. From its cloak he took the Spear of Power and pressed the sharp point against his forehead until his feet were firm on the earth again.

Once more came the music, now towering over him in a great wave of unearthly melody filled with voices calling and crying to him. Almost at the end of his strength, Finn rested his forehead on the point of the spear and was wakened by the sharp pain of it. In the darkness a pale mist was coming over the hills toward Tara. It was Allyn, and Finn saw that he was both beautiful and terrible, like a great bird, but a monster all the same. Allyn drew nearer and nearer, floating over the hills and across the glens while his wondrous music pulsed and beat like a tide over and around Finn. But Finn stood fast, for now he heard too the beating of his own heart, in which flowed the blood of his fathers.

Suddenly a fiery green flame roared from the throat of Allyn and shot toward Tara like a bolt of lightning. Finn raised his crimson cloak and the fire fell against it and died. With a shriek of anger Allyn turned and fled back over the hills toward the Mountain of Cullion, but Finn sped after him, a hill at every leap, a glen at every step, and still the music was around him like a sea. When he reached the river Boyne, Finn dashed a handful of its sacred water over his face and ran on, faster than ever. But Allyn ran slower because he felt behind him the power of someone stronger than he.

Now to the north loomed the crags of the Mountain of Cullion with its door open for the coming of Allyn. The radiance of the fairy palace glowed softly from within the mountain. At the doorway the Fairy Folk called to Allyn in their high sweet voices and urged him on. Yet, like a hound overtaking a stag, Finn gained on his prey. Just as Allyn reached the portal of the mountain, Finn hurled his Spear of Power. It passed through the fog-white body of Allyn, and the Fairy Folk seized it in their hands with cries of triumph. "Our Spear! Our own has come to us!" Then the door in the mountain closed and the brightness was gone. Allyn, pale as a ghost, lay dead on the cold

ground without the mark of a wound on him.

When Finn returned to Tara in the light of morning, he brought with him the head of Allyn and put it on the ramparts. The High King kept his word. He made Finn the leader of the Fianna like his father before him, and he gave honor to the old warriors who had followed Cool Mac Trenmor. Then Conn of the Hundred Battles spoke to all the heroes of Tara.

"If there is any man here who will not pledge his faith to Finn Mac Cool, let him depart out of Ireland." A great shout went up as all the heroes pledged their faith to Finn Mac Cool as Lord of the Fianna, and the first man to grasp his hand was Goll Mac Morna, for he said, "You are a better man than I am, Finn Mac Cool. There is no man like you."

And the glory of Finn grew until he was famed in all Ireland and in Scotland too. The Scottish people called him Fingal. He fought against giants and grew in size until he was a giant himself. Men say that he and the Scottish giants built a great causeway across the sea so that they could visit each other. Once Finn Mac Cool picked up a mountain and hurled it into the sea. The hole that he left in the earth filled with water and is there to this day. It is called Lough Neagh. The mountain fell into the sea and became the Isle of Man. It is the same size and shape as Lough Neagh.

Finn never got his death, for neither time nor doom can kill such a hero. St. Patrick himself knew Finn Mac Cool and he said of him, "He was a king, a seer and a poet. He was a lord with a manifold and great train. He was our magician, our knowledgeable one, our soothsayer. All that he did was sweet with him. And, however ye deem my testimony of Finn excessive, and although ye hold my praising overstrained, nevertheless, and by the King that is above me, he was three times better than all I say."

The Poem of Finn

It is the month of May is the pleasant time; its face is beautiful; the blackbird sings his full song, the living wood is his holding, the cuckoos are singing and ever singing; there is a welcome before the brightness of summer.

Summer is lessening the rivers, the swift horses are looking for the pool; the heath spreads out its long hair, the bog asphodel grows. A wildness comes on the heart of the deer; the sad restless sea is asleep.

Bees with their little strength carry a load reaped from the flowers; the cattle go up muddy to the mountains; the ant has a good full feast.

The harp of the wood is playing music; there is color on the hills, and a haze on the full lakes, and entire peace upon every sail.

The corn-crake is speaking, a loud-voiced poet; the high lonely waterfall is singing a welcome to the warm pool, the talking of the rushes has begun.

The light swallows are darting; the loudness of music is around the hill; there is grass on the trembling bogs.

The bog is as dark as the feathers of the raven; the cuckoo makes a loud welcome; the speckled salmon is leaping; as strong is the leaping of the swift fighting man.

It is pleasant is the color of the time; rough winter is gone; every plentiful wood is white; summer is a joyful peace.

A flock of birds pitches in the meadow; there are sounds in the green fields, there is in them a clear rushing stream.

There is a hot desire on you for the racing of horses; twisted holly makes a leash for the hound; a bright spear has been shot into the earth, and the flag-flower is golden under it.

A little bird is singing at the top of his voice; the lark is singing clear tidings; May without fault, of beautiful colors.

I have another story for you; the ox is lowing, the winter is creeping in, the summer is gone. High and cold the wind, low the sun, cries are about us; the sea is quarreling.

The ferns are reddened and their shape is hidden; the cry of the wild goose is heard; the cold has caught the wings of the birds; it is the time of ice-frost, hard, unhappy.

Dermot in
the Land-under-Wave

Dermot, a hero of the Fianna, was brought up by
Angus Og, son of the Dagda, the Irish god of love.
He lived in a palace on the river Boyne, which takes
its name from Boann, wife of the Dagda. Surrounded
by these powerful forces of love, it is no wonder
that Dermot later stole the love of Finn's wife,
Grania. Dermot, both gentle and generous, was
sensitive to the ideal of honor and for a long while

remained faithful to Finn, in spite of his love for Grania.

Folklorists have much to say about the "loathly lady" who appears in this story. She may represent the woman whose beauty is only revealed when she is loved. She may also represent Royal Rule, the duties of a king, "ugly, brutish, loathly—in the end, beautiful," of which only a hero with a gentle heart can be worthy. Or perhaps, like the Irish banshee, or "fairy woman," she is a spirit of the Other World who has returned from the Land of Death and who for a short while is able to exist through the power of love.

The picture of the Other World as seen in this story is taken from ancient Irish poetry. The magic ship in which Dermot travels to Land-under-Wave is the Ocean Sweeper, belonging to the sea god, Manannan, son of Lir and half brother to the Swan Children.

Dermot's efforts to save his love show his capacity for self-sacrifice. As in the Greek myth of Cupid and Psyche, the mortal must perform heroic deeds to reclaim the immortal loved one whom he has lost through his own folly. But in Dermot's hour of need a helper comes. He is red, a color which means magic, so that we know he comes from the Other World; it is the Dagda himself. The cup of healing and the magic drink of water can be seen in Celtic statues of God the Father, from whom, as Julius Caesar said, "all Gauls pride themselves on being descended."

Of all the Fianna who served under Finn Mac Cool, the youngest was Dermot O'Dyna, slender as a reed, his brown hair falling lightly over his forehead. On his brow was a love spot which made every girl who saw it love him. This handsome boy had a heart to help others, and he was a poet as well, but he was no soft thing. Dermot was a great hunter and warrior. At his side hung a shining sword, and in each hand he carried a spear. When his battle anger came upon him, the red blood glowed in his limbs and the hero light shone around him.

One cold winter night the Fianna returned home from hunting. They warmed themselves at their hearth, lay down in their beds, and each man pulled his cover close.

About midnight there was a knock at the door, and in from the snow came a woman, wild and ugly, wet to the skin, with her hair a mass of tangles down to her heels. She went to Finn and shook him by the shoulder.

"Give me your blanket, Finn Mac Cool." Her voice grated like a rusty hinge. Finn took one look at her, ugly as she was, and pulled his blanket over his head.

The woman gave a screech and turned to Finn's son, Oisin. "Give me your blanket, Oisin, son of Finn." But when Oisin opened his eyes and saw what a hag she was, he turned himself away and wrapped his blanket tighter about him.

The woman screamed again and went to where Dermot was lying in his bed close to the hearth. "Give me your blanket, Dermot O'Dyna," said she.

Dermot looked up at the woman. "You're as ugly as sin with your hair down to your heels, but I'll give you my blanket for all that," said he, and he gave it to her. His brown hair fell back from his forehead, so that she saw the love spot.

"Dermot," she said, "I've been gone from my home for seven years and this is the first night I've had a roof over my head. Let me have your place by the fire."

Dermot moved his bed back from the hearth. "You're a dreadful sight, but that's no matter," he said. "Take my place by the fire."

Before long she asked, "Dermot O'Dyna, will you give me your bed?"

"You want too much," said Dermot. "First my blanket, then my place by the fire, and now it's my bed you're wanting. But you've enough troubles on that ugly head of yours already. Take the bed." Then he got up and she lay down with his blanket around her, close to the fire. And Dermot sat up for the rest of the night with his back against the wall.

While it was still dark, he came to his bed. And what he saw there by the light of the fire was a beautiful young woman, and she asleep, wrapped in a cloak the color of a dark sea wave. He called the others to look at her and said, "Is not this the most beautiful woman that ever was seen?"

"She is that," they said, and they went away softly, not to waken her.

Before dawn she stirred and rose from the bed. "Are you awake, Dermot?" she said, in a voice like honey. And he came to her, saying, "I am awake."

Then she said, "If you could have your wish for the best house that ever was built, where would it be?"

"On the green hillside looking out to sea," said Dermot.

"Take your bed now and sleep," said she.

Dermot slept until broad daylight. Then two men of the Fianna woke him and said, "We are after seeing a great house on the green hillside where there was none before."

And the strange woman said, "Rise up, Dermot. Do not be lying there, but look out and see your house."

So he looked out, and when he saw the great house standing ready, he said, "I will go to it if you will come along with me."

"I will do that," she said, "if you will promise never to say how I looked when I came to you."

"I will never say it to you forever," said Dermot.

They went up then to the house, and it was ready for them, with food and servants. And everything they could wish for, they had. But after three days she said, "You care more for hounds and hunting than for any woman in the world. You are missing your comrades of the Fianna."

"I do not miss them," said Dermot.

But she said, "Go to them, and you will find me here when you come back."

"Who will take care of my greyhound and her three pups?" said he.

"Have no fear for them," she said.

So Dermot went back to hunt with the Fianna and they gave him a great welcome, though they were envious that he had got the great house and the beautiful woman they themselves had turned away.

Now while Dermot was gone, Finn Mac Cool went to the house and saw the woman standing at the door in a kirtle of sea-green silk. "Are you vexed with me, Queen?" he said.

"I am not, indeed," she said. "You are welcome and there is no request you would not get in this house."

"Will you give me one of the pups of Dermot's greyhound?" said Finn Mac Cool.

"That is no great thing to ask," she said. And she gave him the pup.

At the fall of night when Dermot came back to the house, his greyhound gave a yelp and he saw that one of the pups was gone. Then Dermot guessed what the woman had done. He was angry and said to her, "If you had brought to mind how you looked when I gave you my bed,

and your hair hanging to your feet, you would not have given away the pup."

"That's once," said she, "and you ought not to say that, Dermot."

"I ask your pardon for saying it," said Dermot. And they forgave one another.

The next day Dermot went back to the Fianna and the woman stayed at the house. And she put on a blue cloak that sparkled like the sea under a golden sun. After a while she saw Oisin coming toward her and she gave him welcome. When he asked for one of the greyhound's pups, she gave it to him and he took it away.

That night when Dermot came back, the greyhound met him and howled twice. Then he knew that another of the pups was gone. He looked at the woman and he said to the greyhound, "If she had remembered the way she looked when she came to me, she would not have given the pup away."

"That's twice," said the woman.

The next day while Dermot was off with the Fianna, Goll Mac Morna came to the house, and there stood the woman in a gown that flashed with light like waves in a setting sun. Goll Mac Morna got one of the pups, the same as the others. When Dermot came back that night, the greyhound gave three terrible yelps, the saddest that ever were heard, and Dermot saw that all the pups were gone. Then his anger came upon him and he said, "If this woman had remembered how she was when I found her, with her hair in tangles down to her heels, she would not have let the pup go."

"That's three," said the woman. And on the moment the house was gone and the woman with it. The greyhound lay dead at Dermot's feet. Then a great sorrow settled on him and he set off to search for the beautiful woman.

When he had traveled a day and a night, he met with a cowherd. "Did you see a beautiful woman going this way?" asked Dermot.

"I did that," said the cowherd, "early in the morning of yesterday, and she walking fast down the path to the shore."

So Dermot followed the path to the water's edge; and there he saw a ship, its sails spread and no man in it. The ship was none too near, but he took a run, leaned on a spear, and vaulted into the ship. And it sailed on, all of itself.

The sea grew rough and wild, the waves were mountain-high, but the little ship climbed the billows and plunged into the deeps. Watery peaks towered above Dermot, higher and higher, now green, now blue, now fiery silver. Then in the cavern between the waves the voice of the sea sounded around him, and far above, he saw the waters close like a great pearly shell. They hung suspended and trembling, but they did not fall.

And all at once the little ship was gone. Dermot found himself standing on a flowery plain, bathed in the rainbow light of spring. He walked forward through the meadow. He breathed the honey sweetness of clover and of blossoms on silver boughs. It was the Land-under-Wave, a lovely land older than the world, yet ever young, a land on which many flowers rained down. Horses of golden yellow were there on the meadow, other horses of purple color, and still others the color of the blue sky. And the pure sea surrounded all that Land-under-Wave.

As Dermot walked, he saw before him a drop of blood, ruby-red in the grass. "It is the blood of my greyhound," he said, and he took it up in a napkin. When he had gone farther, he came to a drop of blood red as a wild strawberry under the leaves, and this too he took in the napkin. Where the grass turned to rushes beside his path, he found yet a third drop of blood, deep red as a cherry in summer. "This too I must take," said Dermot. "Surely it is the blood of my greyhound."

Then he saw a woman cutting rushes like a mad thing. "What is this place?" asked Dermot, for as yet he knew nothing of it.

"It is Land-under-Wave," said she.

"And what use have you for the rushes?"

"The king's daughter is come home," she said. "She was seven years away and under spells. Now she lies sick and must die, but she longs to lie once more on a bed of green rushes."

Then Dermot knew who was the king's daughter in Land-under-Wave, and he said, "I will not let her die. Show me where she is."

"There is only one way to do that," said she. "You cannot go by yourself. I will cover you with rushes and carry you there on my back." And though it went against his pride, he let the woman put the rushes around him and carry him, rushes and all, to the room where the king's daughter lay. When she put down the rushes, out he stepped from the greenness of them, and the daughter of

King-under-Wave looked up from her bed and put her hands in his.

"The worst of my sickness is gone from me now that I see you," she said. "But, oh Dermot, I thought of you three times on my journey to this place, and each time I lost a drop of my heart's blood."

"I have them," said Dermot. "Take them in a drink of clear water and you will be well again."

"That is not so easy," she said. "I must drink them from a cup of healing that is held by the king of the Plain of Wonder, and no man ever got it or ever will get it."

"Tell me where to find that cup," said Dermot. "There are not enough men on the ridge of the world to keep it from me."

"Between that country and mine there runs only a little river," said she. "But narrow as that river seems, you would have to sail across it for a year and a day to reach the Plain of Wonder."

"Still, I will try," said Dermot. "I may be lucky." And he set off until he came to the little river. At first he saw no way to cross it, but as he walked by the river's edge, he saw a red-haired man standing waist-deep in the water. His skin was red and his eyes burned red as coals of fire.

"Dermot of the Brown Hair, you need help," said the man. "Put your foot in my hand and I will give you a lift across the river." Dermot did as the red man bade him and in one leap he was across the river. "Now," said the red man, "you need the cup that belongs to the king of the Plain of Wonder. I will go with you."

They went on together until they came to the king's castle. Then Dermot called out that the cup of healing should be sent to him or else champions should be sent out to fight him. The king did not send the cup, but he sent twice eight hundred fighting men, and in three hours not one was left to stand against Dermot. Still the king did not send the cup, but he sent twice nine hundred champions to fight Dermot. Within four hours, not one was left standing.

Then the king himself came and stood in his great door and called out, "Who is this man who fights my armies singlehanded?"

"I will tell you that," said Dermot. "I am a man of the Fianna of Ireland."

"You might have told me that before," said the king. "I would not have wasted my men upon you. What did you say you wanted?"

"The cup of healing I am asking," said Dermot.

"No man ever got that cup from me," said the king, "but I will give it to you, whether or not there is healing in it."

He gave Dermot the cup and they parted in friendship. Then Dermot went on till he came to the river. He put his foot in the palm of the red man's hand and leaped lightly across.

"I know where it is you are going," said the red man. "It is to heal the daughter of King-under-Wave. When you go to her, give her clear water from that cup and a drop of her blood in it. Do this three times and her sickness will be gone. But there is another thing will be gone, and that is the love you have for her."

"That will not go from me," said Dermot.

"It will go from you," said the red man. "And make no secret of it, for she will know and her father will know. King-under-Wave will offer you great riches for healing his daughter. But take nothing from him except a ship to bring you home again to Ireland. You will find your greyhound alive and well on the hearthstone of the Fianna."

"You have the second sight. Who are you, then?" asked Dermot.

"I am the messenger from the Other World," said the red man. "I come to the help of those who have a heart to help others."

Dermot did as the red man bade him. He brought to the daughter of King-under-Wave clear water and the three drops of blood in the cup of healing. She drank and was healed. But no sooner had she drunk the last drop than Dermot's love for her was gone. She knew it and the king knew it.

Still, his daughter was healed and there was no more lamenting. The palace of King-under-Wave was filled with music. As for Dermot, he asked for a ship to bring him home to Ireland, and the moment he set foot on earth, he saw his greyhound, alive and well, running toward him through the golden gorse. He heard the hunting horn of Finn and saw the Fianna coming over the green hills to greet him with a hundred thousand welcomes.

Tam Lin

In the Western Isles of Scotland a festival for the
fairies used to be held at Halloween. The Scottish
Halloween festival was meant to guard against and
to placate the fairies, who on that night, the last
night of the year in the old Celtic calendar, sometimes released those they had stolen away. The doors
of fairy dwellings in the hills would open, and the
fairies, who had once been the Celtic gods, came

riding out. The great god Lugh had ridden with a whole
Fairy Cavalry, and Manannan had had a steed, Splendid
Mane, who could gallop over land or sea. The fairies of
Scotland loved nothing better than to ride in procession.
Whether their horses were black, brown, or white, their
step was lighter than the wind, and as swift.

In the ballad of Tam Lin, when the hero falls asleep
under an apple tree, it is no wonder that the Fairy Queen
finds him quickly, for the apple tree, whether it grows in
the Biblical Garden of Eden, in the Greek Garden of the
Hesperides, in Avalon, the Celtic Happy Isle, or at the
gates of Fairyland, means that the Other World is near at
hand.

As in "Beauty and the Beast," the plucking of a rose is
the signal for the enchanted hero to appear, and in both
stories the power of love releases him from an evil spell.
This theme of redemption is one of the great ideas of
mythology and of religion. The Fairy Queen changes Tam
Lin into dangerous and horrifying shapes in order to make
Burd Janet let him go, but love proves stronger than all
the powers of Fairyland.

Burd Janet would always do as she liked. She was as will-ful a lass as ever set foot from her father's hall. When she was told, "Go not into the woods," into the woods she was bound to go. And so it was, on a night when the old nurse called around her the four-and-twenty fair ladies who were playing at chess in the great hall.

"Go not into the woods," whispered the old woman. "Tam Lin has been seen again at the well."

There was not a lady but knew of Tam Lin, the son of a high-born earl. Tam Lin had been gone from home these seven long years, no one knew where. But on certain nights he would appear by the old well in the woods, and girls who went to draw water at the well on those nights swore that the handsome young man had cast a spell on them.

From one he might take a ring, from another her green mantle, and sometimes he stole a kiss. "Now and again, he steals the girl herself," said the old nurse.

At this, some of the ladies shivered, while others only laughed and blushed. But none of them dared try their luck at the well in the woods, except Burd Janet. She braided her yellow hair, tucked her green skirt up to her knees, and ran off from her father's hall into the woods as fast as she could hie.

When she came to the well, all was silent and still, but she saw the shadowy form of a milk-white horse cropping the grass in the moonlight. His fore hoofs were shod with silver, his hind hoofs with gleaming gold, but he stepped so lightly that he left no print on the grass.

Looking about, this way and that, Burd Janet smelled the scent of roses and came upon a low bush in full bloom close by the old well. She picked a rose. She picked another. And suddenly young Tam Lin stood before her, kilted and bonneted like any mortal man, but pale as a ghost, and saying in such a voice as made her tremble, "Lady, you must take no more roses. And why did you come here without asking leave of me?"

Janet was ever a lass with a will of her own. She looked at him straight and said, "I may come here when I like, for these woods are my father's and I am his heir." But before the words were out of her mouth, she was in the power of Tam Lin and had no more will of her own.

"What are you?" she whispered then. "Are you an earthly knight? Were you christened in chapel like any man born of woman?"

When Tam Lin spoke again, his voice was full of sorrow. "I was born of woman, but alas, I am no longer an earthly knight. One luckless day, a bitter day, as I turned home from hunting, a cold north wind began to blow and a strange drowsiness came over me. I fell from my horse and lay in a swoon under an apple tree. There the Queen of the Fairies found me, for it was she who had sent the Fairy Sleep upon me. She carried me away to dwell with her in yonder green hill, which is the entrance to Fairyland. Pleasant it is in that land. Old age does not follow youth in Fairyland. There are fine temples with pillars of glass, and palaces of gold and silver, trees laden with fruits and flowers. The air is full of birds of the sweetest song and most brilliant colors. All night long there is dancing to the tune of pipes and harps. But every seven years the fairies must send a tribute to hell, and this year I fear they will send me."

"It must not be, Tam Lin," said Janet. "Tell me true, how can I save you?"

Then Tam Lin touched Burd Janet's long green sleeve and took her by the hand. "Tomorrow night is Halloween when the elfin court will ride—through Scotland, through England, and around the world. At sunset the doors of the fairy hill will open and the whole court will ride forth. At midnight they will reach the pool at Miles Cross.

Sprinkle a ring of holy water around you, Janet, and wait by that pool. First will come the king and queen, riding on black horses. Let them pass. Then come the maidens, footmen, grooms, and squires. Their horses are brown. Let them pass. Last come the knights on milk-white steeds. I will be with them."

"How shall I know you from all the others?" asked Janet.

"Watch for my horse, for his nostrils breathe fiery flame. And watch for my right hand. It will be gloved, and my left hand bare. Watch for my crown. The queen has set a golden star in it, because I was once an earthly man."

"What must I do when I see you?"

"Pull me down from my milk-white steed and let the bridle fall. Then cast your green cloak over me and never let me go. The fairies will change my shape to steal me away again. But hold me fast, and when I change at last into a mother-naked man, dip me in the pool." The voice of Tam Lin faded and the woods grew dim with mist. Burd Janet saw and heard no more. Tam Lin and his milk-white steed were gone.

When Janet came to her father's hall again, she looked

as fine as any queen, but strange and pale.

"You have been with Tam Lin," cried an elder knight. "I can see it. Tam Lin has put his spell on you." And all the ladies left their games of chess to stare at Janet.

But she was ever a lass with a will of her own, and answered, "Hold your tongue, old man. I would not give my elfin knight for any knight in my father's hall." And she spoke no other word to any man or maid.

The next night, the night of Halloween, away she went again, wearing her green cloak and carrying a cup of holy water in her hand. Black was the night and gloomy was the way, until she came to the pool at Miles Cross. There she made a ring of holy water and stood within it. About the dead of the night, a north wind began to blow. It whistled through the reeds, it moaned in the hemlocks. And above the wind Burd Janet heard the jingle of silver bridle bells and the eerie singing of many voices. Louder and louder grew the sound as the fairy court came riding, with a will-o'-the-wisp twinkling before them to light the path.

Now the troop of fairies came in sight, led by the king and queen. They wore purple tunics, with green hoods over their heads and silver clasps around their wrists. They rode on black horses. Janet stood still and let them pass. Then the maidens, the footmen, grooms, and squires rode by, each on a horse of brown. She let them pass.

Last came the knights, all crowned with gold and riding on milk-white steeds. She saw a horse whose nostrils shot forth fiery flame. The rider's right hand was gloved, his left hand bare, and the crown on his head was tipped with a golden star. Janet gripped the bridle and pulled the rider down.

Then the fairy people saw Burd Janet with Tam Lin in her arms, and there arose a weird cry from all the company. The fairy queen shrieked, "Tam Lin's gone from me!" and with that, began to work her wicked spells. As Janet held Tam Lin, he turned into a crawling, scaly lizard, then into a hissing, twisting snake. But all the while Janet heard her lover's voice, "If you would be mine, hold me fast, let me not pass."

He turned into a raging lion, but still Janet held him in her arms. He turned into a snarling wolf, but she heard his own voice say, "Hold me fast, let me not go." Then he appeared in her arms like a wild deer with antlers sharp as

spears, and again his shape changed and he became a burning coal. But all the while Burd Janet held him fast, and he did her no harm.

At last she felt in her arms the form of a perfect man, a warm and living, earthly man, and she dipped him in the pool. From the queen of the fairies came an angry wail. "He's won! Cursed be the fair face of her who has stolen away the bonniest knight in all my company. If I had known what I know tonight, Tam Lin, I would have taken away your gray eyes and given you eyes of wood. If I had known you would love that girl instead of me, I would have taken away your heart and given you a heart of stone."

Suddenly the fairy troop was gone and Burd Janet was left alone with her true love. She took him by the hand and he led her home to her father's hall. Then through all Scotland the word went out, and the tale was told of the brave lass who dared at dark midnight on Halloween to save her lover's soul. Though you would search the wide world over, they say, you will never find another pair like Burd Janet and young Tam Lin.

To the Sun

Greeting to you, sun of the seasons, as you travel the skies on high, with your strong steps on the wing of the heights; you are the happy mother of the stars.

You sink down in the perilous ocean without harm and without hurt; you rise up on the quiet wave like a young queen in flower.

Scottish Gaelic. Traditional folk prayer

To the New Moon

Greeting to you, new moon, kindly jewel of guidance!
I bend my knees to you, I offer you my love.

I bend my knees to you, I raise my hands to you, I lift up
my eye to you, new moon of the seasons.

Greeting to you, new moon, darling of my love! Greeting
to you, new moon, darling of graces.

You journey on your course, you steer the flood-tides, you
light up your face for us, new moon of the seasons.

Queen of guidance, queen of good luck, queen of my love,
new moon of the seasons!

Scottish Gaelic. Traditional folk prayer

The Lad of Luck and the Monster of the Loch

As the centuries passed, the gods of Celtic mythology became the more familiar fairies and giants of folklore. The people still told tales of Cuchulain, of Finn, and other godlike heroes, but the sons of humble Irish and Scottish herdsmen and fishermen knew that the blood of these heroes flowed in their own veins. They too could perform great feats.

Like the old gods, the Scottish hero of this story

has a supernatural horse and hound. He is as strong as Cuchulain and has to try several swords before he finds one that does not break under his mighty blows. His sword comes from a mysterious smith who is clearly the Gubbaun Saor, the Celtic equivalent of the Greek Hephaestus who helped to make human beings at the creation of the world, and who had the gift of prophecy.

As shown in the old maps, oceans and lakes have always been the homes of terrifying, often evil creatures. As the Greek Hercules fought the nine-headed Hydra, and as Perseus saved the princess Andromeda from a sea monster, so the Lad of Luck fought the Monster of the Loch. St. Michael and St. George fighting against their dragons, or Thor fighting the Midgard Serpent, are no more heroic than the Lad of Luck.

Although the story has its roots in Celtic myths about the early days of the world, it is full of humor. This version is adapted from a tale included in J. F. Campbell's Popular Tales of the West Highlands. It was told by a fisherman named John Mackenzie, who lived near Inveraray in 1859.

In days long gone, there was a poor old fisherman who lived between the sea and the loch. One year he was not getting much fish and he and his poor old wife were going hungry.

On a day of days, and he fishing in the sea, there rose a mermaid at the side of his boat. Her eyes were sea-green, her long golden hair floated on the waves, and below her waist there was a flash of silver like the scales of a fish.

"What would you give me to send you plenty of fish?" said she.

"Ach," said the old man, "I have not much to give."

"Then I must have your first son."

"I would give you that, if I had a son," he said, "but my wife and I are grown too old to have children."

"What do you have, then?"

"All I have in the world is my old mare, my old dog, my old wife, and myself."

"Then take these," said the mermaid, and she put nine seeds into his hand. "Give three of these seeds to your wife, three to the dog, and three to the mare. In their own good time, your wife will have three sons, the mare three foals, and the dog three puppies. And from now on, you will catch plenty of fish."

The fisherman thanked the mermaid and started to row to shore.

"Hold on a bit," said she. "Remember, I must have your first son. Bring him to me when he is three years old." The fisherman promised to do so.

Everything happened as the mermaid said, but when the end of three years was nearing, the old man grew sorrowful and heavyhearted. When the day came to keep his promise, he went to fish as usual, but he did not take his first son with him.

The mermaid rose at the side of the boat and asked, "Did you bring your son to me?"

"Och, I forgot that this was the day," said the fisherman.

"Did you, indeed?" said the mermaid. "Well, you shall have four more years to see if it be easier for you to part with him then."

The fisherman went home full of glee that he had got four more years of his son, and he kept on catching plenty of fish. But at the end of the four years, sorrow and woe struck him again, and he took not a meal, nor did a turn of work. His wife could not think what was ailing him.

When the day came, he went to fish as before, and the

mermaid rose at the side of the boat and said, "Did you bring your son to me?"

"Och, I forgot him this time too," said the old man.

"Go home then," said the mermaid. "You may have your son for seven more years, but this will not make it easier for you to part with him."

The old man was full of joy. He thought that he himself would be dead before the seven years passed, and he need never see the mermaid again. But the end of those seven years came, and the old man still lived. He could rest neither day nor night, and the eldest son asked his father if anything was troubling him. The old man said that he could not tell. The lad said he *must* know. And at last his father told him how the matter was between him and the mermaid.

"Let the blacksmith make me a great strong sword," said the lad. "I will go to seek my fortune away from the sea where the mermaid will not find me."

His father went to the smithy and came home with a sword. The lad gave it a shake or two and it went in a hundred splinters. He asked for another sword twice as heavy, but it broke in two halves. Back went the old man to the smithy, and the smith made such a sword he never made the like of it before. The son gave it a shake or two and said, "This will do. It's high time now to travel on my way."

The next morning he put a saddle on his black horse and took the world for his pillow. His black dog was by his side.

When he went on a bit, he saw a great dog, a falcon, and an otter fighting over the carcass of a sheep beside the road. He took his sword and divided the sheep, three shares to the dog, two shares to the otter, and one share to the falcon, so that they stopped fighting and ate in peace.

"For this," said the dog, "if swiftness of foot or sharpness of teeth will give you aid, remember me, and I will be at your side."

Said the otter, "If swimming deep under water will help you, remember me, and I will be at your side."

Said the falcon, "Where swiftness of wing or crook of a claw will help you, think of me, and I will be at your side."

The lad thanked them and went on until he came to a king's house. There he took work as a cowherd, and his wages were to be according to the milk the cattle gave. But the grass was scarce, and when he took the cows home in the evening, they had not much milk to give, and he had not much supper.

The next day he took the cows farther and found fine grass in a green glen. But about the time when he should drive the cattle home, who came roaring out of a great house but a giant with a sword in his hand.

"HUI! HAU! HOGARAICH!!!" said the giant. "These cattle are mine. They are on my land. And you are a dead man."

"That is easy to say," said the lad.

To grips they went—himself and the giant. The lad drew his great clean-sweeping sword, the black dog leaped on the giant's back, and in a twinkling the giant lost his head. The lad found gold and silver in the giant's house, and fine armor that the giant had taken from the men he had killed.

"I might need that," said the lad, and he took it. And when the cattle were milked that night, there *was* milk.

But after a time the glen grew bare of grass. The lad thought he would go a little farther, and he came to a great park. The cows were only a short time grazing there when a great wild giant came, full of rage and madness. "HUI! HAW! HOAGRAICH!!!" said the giant. "A drink of your blood will quench my thirst this night."

"That's easy to say," said the lad. And at each other they went. *There* was a shaking of blades. But just as it seemed the giant would get the victory, the cowherd called his black dog. The dog caught the giant by the neck, and the cowherd struck off his head. The lad went home very tired that night, but the king's cattle gave so much milk that his whole family was delighted they had got such a cowherd.

But one night when he came home, all were at crying and woe. The dairymaid said that a great beast with three heads was in the loch and every year the beast was given someone to eat. This year the lot had fallen on the king's daughter. The only hope was a great hero who had come to rescue the princess.

"What hero is that?" said the cowherd.

"Oh, he is a great general," said the dairymaid, "and if he rescues the princess, he will marry her, for the king has promised to give her to anyone who will kill the beast."

On the morrow, the king's daughter and the great general went to the black hill at the upper end of the loch to meet the monster. They were but a short time there when the beast stirred and raised its three heads in the midst of the loch. The general, seeing this terror of a beast, took fright and slunk away and hid himself. And the king's daughter was under fear and trembling, with no one at all to save her.

Then she saw a handsome youth riding a black horse and coming to where she was. He was marvelously arrayed, and fully armed, and his black dog moved after him.

"There is gloom on your face, girl," said the young champion. "What are you doing here?"

"Oh, that's no matter," said the king's daughter. "It's not long I'll be here at all events."

"We'll see about that," said he.

"It is so," said she. "I am about to be eaten by the monster of the loch, and a warrior, as worthy as you, fled from it not long since."

"He is worthy who stands the war," said the youth. Then he lay down to sleep and said, "Rouse me if you see the beast making for shore."

"How would I rouse you?" she asked.

"Put your gold ring on my little finger."

They were not long there when she saw the beast making for shore. She took a ring off her finger and put it on the little finger of the lad. He awoke and went into the water with his sword and his dog to meet the monster. But there was spluttering and splashing between himself and the beast! The dog was doing all he might, and the king's daughter was shaking with fear at the noise of the beast. They would now be under the water, and now above. But at last the lad cut one of the heads off the monster. It gave one roar, "RAIVIC!" and the rocks echoed its screech. Then it drove the loch in a spindrift of spray from end to end, and in a twinkling it went out of sight.

"Good luck and victory were following you, lad!" said the king's daughter. "I am safe for one night, but the beast will come again and forever, until the other two heads come off it."

He caught the head he had cut off and strung it on a loop of willow. Then he told the princess to carry it home and bring it back tomorrow. But she had not gone far when the great general saw her and said that he would kill her if she would not say that 'twas he took the head off the beast.

"Oh!" says she. "I will say it. Who else took the head off the beast but you!" They reached the king's house, the general carrying the beast's head on his shoulder. Then there was rejoicing, and on the morrow, when they went back to the loch, there was no question at all but that this hero of a general would save the king's daughter.

They were not long there when the fearful beast stirred in the midst of the loch, and the general slunk away as before. But soon came the man of the black horse, dressed more grandly than yesterday. No matter, the princess knew it was the very same lad.

"I am pleased to see you," said she. "I am in hopes you will handle your great sword today as you did yesterday. Come up and take breath."

Before long, they saw the beast steaming in the midst of the loch. The lad lay down and he said, "If I sleep before the beast comes this way, rouse me."

"How would I rouse you?"

"Put your earring in my ear."

He had barely fallen asleep when the king's daughter cried, "Rouse! Rouse!" But wake he would not, until she took the earring out of her ear and put it in his. At once he woke, and went to meet the beast. But *there* was Tloopersteich and Tlaperstich, rawceil s'tawceil, spluttering, splashing, raving, and roaring on the beast!

They kept on thus for a long time, and just as night was coming, the lad cut off another head. He strung it on the strand of willow, leaped on the black horse, and went back to herding the cattle.

When the king's daughter went home with the heads, the general met her and said she must tell it was he who took the head off the beast this time also.

"Who else?" said she. And when they reached the king's house there was joy and gladness. The king was now sure that this great general would save his daughter, for the last head would certainly be off the beast on the morrow.

But the third day when the king's daughter betook herself to the bank of the loch, the general hid himself from the monster. Then the hero of the black horse came. He took a nap while they waited for the monster to come near the shore, and the king's daughter woke him by putting her other earring in his other ear.

If rawceil and s'tawceil, roaring and raving were on the beast before, this day it was horrible. But no matter, the cowherd took the third head off the beast and strung it on the willow strand. The king's daughter went home with the heads and the general was to marry her the next day.

"I will marry no one but the man who can take the heads off the willow strand without cutting the willow," said she.

"That would be the man that put the heads on it," said the king.

The general tried, but he could not loose them. There was no one about the house who could loose them. Only the cowherd had not tried yet. When he was sent for, he was not long in throwing the heads hither and thither.

"But stop a bit, my lad," said the king's daughter. "The man that took the heads off the beast, he has my ring and my two earrings."

The cowherd took them from his pocket and threw them on the table.

"You are my man," said the king's daughter, and they married that same night, and everything going on well.

But one day they were sauntering by the side of the loch and there came a beast more wonderfully terrible than the other, and takes the lad away to the bottom of the loch without fear, or asking. The king's daughter was now mournful, tearful, blind-sorrowful for her married man. Then came the old smith who had made her hero's great sword, and she told him all. He advised her to spread her finest things in the very same place where the beast took away her man. And so she did.

The beast put up its nose and said, "Fine is thy jewelry, king's daughter."

"Finer yet is the jewel you took from me," said she. "Deliver him to me and you shall have all you see here." The beast threw the lad alive and well on the bank of the loch, took the pretty things, and was gone.

A short time after this, the same beast took away the king's daughter. Her man was mournful, tearful, wandering up and down the banks of the loch, by day and night. The old smith met him and told him there was but the one way of killing the beast, and this was it. "In the island in the midst of the loch is a white-footed hind of the slenderest legs and the swiftest step. If the hind should be caught, there would spring out of her a crow. If the crow should be caught, there would spring out of her a trout. But there is an egg in the mouth of the trout, and the soul of the loch monster is in the egg. If the egg breaks, the beast is dead."

Now the beast would sink each boat that went on the loch. So the lad leaped over the water to the island on his black horse, and his black dog with one bound came after him. He saw the white-footed hind, but his own dog could not catch her. Then the lad remembered the great dog who

had promised to help him with swiftness of foot and sharpness of tooth. No sooner thought than the generous dog
was at his side. He took after the hind and was not long in
bringing her to earth. But he no sooner caught her than a
crow sprang out of her.

" 'Tis now I need the falcon gray, of sharpest eye and
swiftest wing!" No sooner said than the falcon was after
the crow and put her to earth. But as the crow fell on the
bank of the loch, out of her jumps the trout, and into the
water.

"Oh, that you were by me, otter!" No sooner said than
the otter was at his side. Into the loch she leaped and
brings back the trout. The egg came out of the trout's
mouth and the lad put his foot on it. 'Twas then the beast
let out a roar. "Break not the egg and I will give all you
ask!"

"Give me back my wife," says the lad.

In the wink of an eye she was by his side. But as the lad
got hold of her in both his hands, he let his foot down on
the egg, and there was the beast lying dead before them.
It was horrible to look upon. There were heads above and
heads below, hundreds of heads, and eyes, and five hundred feet.

No matter, they left it there, and they went home. The lad told the king how it was he who had killed the giant, and there was delight and smiling in the king's house that night. The king put great honor on the lad, and he was a great man with the king, who was growing old. When the king died, the lad was crowned in his place. He sent gold and silver home to his old father and mother and his two brothers. And if they have not died since then, they are alive to this very day.

The Bells of Ys

In the sixth century, many Britons crossed the sea from Devon and Cornwall to Brittany, "Little Britain." They became the Bretons, but they were still as Celtic as those who stayed in Britain. They brought with them their Druidic religion and their myths, giving new names to places and persons. Cornwall became Cornouailles. King Arthur killed a giant at Mont-Saint-Michel. Morgan le Fay,

Arthur's half sister, who had the gift of death and who was a water spirit, became Dahut in "The Bells of Ys."

Even before the time of the Druids, there had been a Cornish legend about Lyonnesse, a lost island that lay deep under the water between Lands End and the Scilly Islands. And in the Aran Islands off the west coast of Ireland, they still tell of Hy-Brasil, an island which rises from the sea every seven years. In the story told here, Lyonnesse becomes Ys, and like Hy-Brasil, it sometimes rises from the sea.

Sailors off both the Cornish and the Breton coasts say that they have hauled up doors and window frames from the sea's depths, and even submarine forests have been discovered. In these once submerged cities and forests, gods and goddesses roamed, and stories such as "The Bells of Ys" are like the pieces of wood that float up from time to time. In John Updike's words, the glitter is Christian salt, but the wood is pagan.

On the Île de Sein, which appears in the story of Ys, there lived nine Druidesses, who gathered herbs, mixed them with sea foam, and then boiled them for a year and a day. This sacred potion gave inspiration to Druid bards who sang in praise of the Celtic past. They told the story *of Ys so well that even in our own day the mythical tale has inspired an opera, "Le Roi d'Ys" by Lalo, and the haunting "Cathédrale Engloutie" by Debussy.*

At the westernmost tip of Brittany, where the extreme limit of French land narrows to a point, a great cliff faces the fury of the Atlantic Ocean. Here, at the Pointe du Raz, the land and the sea are enemies. In time of storm, monstrous waves, fifty, sixty, even eighty feet high, tear hungrily at the rocks, as if to devour them, and even in calm weather, the Breton sailor prays, "Help me, O Lord, at the Pointe du Raz. My boat is so small and the sea so big."

But once, long ago, on the shore at the Pointe du Raz, there stood a fair and beautiful city called Ys. It was built of stone to last forever, and it was a city of bells. From the stone towers of Ys the bells rang sweetly and softly, marking the hours, calling the people to worship, and warning them in time of danger. In those times there was always danger, and Ys was ringed with a stone wall to protect the city from its enemies by land or by sea. The sea itself was an enemy, for the tides were very fierce and strong on this coast. Without the protection of the wall, the city would have been overwhelmed by the waves. Two gates pierced the wall, one facing the land and one facing the sea, but only when the tide fell, and the sea drew back, could the gate toward the sea be opened.

Gralon, the king of Ys, was a good man. From his high palace he loved to look down on his beautiful city, and he loved even more to look at his beautiful daughter, Dahut. She was a strange child. Her eyes were as blue as the sea and as cold as the sea. Dahut's hair was pale, like the foam that crested on the waves and spread itself on the yellow sands. And as she grew older, her temper became as changeable as the moods of the sea. Dahut could bewitch a man's heart with one toss of her fair hair, one look from her deep eyes.

Some folk said that Dahut *was* a witch, for she often visited the Île de Sein. That rocky islet could barely be seen on the far horizon, and no one lived there except for nine Druidesses. The people of Ys feared these old women, for they were known to gather herbs, mix them with sea foam, and brew them into a potion of magic power.

Ys had reason to fear and hate Dahut. Every young man

who looked at her longed for her, and to love Dahut meant death itself. Every night she sent a masked henchman to the house of some luckless young man, bringing an invitation to visit Dahut in her palace. None of her lovers ever returned. One by one, they were strangled and their bodies were flung over a cliff into a deep gully.

Near the city lived a hermit, who came to King Gralon and warned him that the wickedness of Dahut would bring Ys to ruin and destruction. "Remember, O King, how it is written, 'If thy heart offend thee, cut out thy heart and cast it from thee.'"

But the king trusted his heart. He could think no evil of his beautiful daughter. Even when the people showed him the bodies of their dead sons, he would only pray for Dahut. He would not control her.

Indeed, the king *could* not control Dahut. As a child, she had found her true love, the sea itself, the only lover strong enough to please her. Therefore, Dahut despised all men. Their weakness, compared with the strength of the sea, amused her. This was the secret of her wickedness.

Now, in spite of King Gralon's love for his daughter, he too had a secret which he had never told her. Except for the king, only one young man knew where the key to the gate in the sea wall was hidden. Like Dahut, this young man, Gavin, had one love, but where her love was the sea, his was the city of Ys. Because he was a hunchback, he did not hope for the love of any woman. Instead, the lonely Gavin turned his thoughts to the beauty of Ys, the whiteness of her towers, the sweetness of her bells. Faithful to the trust the king had given him, Gavin kept the key to the sea wall next to his heart.

One spring night, a night of high tide, Dahut walked through the streets of Ys. Above her the bells chimed the hour of midnight and the moonlight shone silver on the sleeping city. But the beauty of the hour meant nothing to Dahut. Ys was only a city of men, all weak and worthless. The sea was calling to her.

Swift as the wind, she passed through the narrow streets of the city and climbed to the top of the sea wall. There stood the bent figure of a young man. It was Gavin, who often came alone at midnight to look down like a guardian on the city he loved.

Dahut came close to him and spoke his name. Gavin bowed with respect and waited for her orders. To Dahut this was only another weak young man, another victim. "Look at me," she commanded.

Then Gavin saw the eyes of Dahut, glittering like cold flame as the waves glittered under the moonlight. She turned and looked down at the city, and Gavin was afraid, not for himself but for Ys. Without thinking, he put his hands to his heart, and at once, by the power of Druid magic, Dahut knew that the key to the sea wall was hidden there.

She put her arms around him, but there was no warmth in them and he tried to free himself. "Give me the key," she whispered.

Then he felt Dahut's cold fingers at his throat, tighter and tighter, strangling him. The key was in her hand and with failing strength he tried to wrest it from her. Then a mist covered his eyes. Gavin heard the bells of Ys ringing for the last time as Dahut threw his body into the sea.

Down the steps she ran from the top of the sea wall to its gate. She thrust the key into the lock, turned it, and pushed with all her force against the heavy gate. Slowly it opened. The tide was rising; already the black water covered the sands. It surged roaring through the open gate and into the city streets. Dahut ran back toward her father's palace, and behind her raced the sea.

The people of Ys began to waken at the sound of the waters. The bell ringer pealed a warning, but it was too late. Only on the higher ground where the king's palace stood was there any hope of escape. From a tower window King Gralon looked out and saw the wild sea raging over the city. He ran to his stable, mounted his swift horse Morwark, and set spurs to its sides. Then above the thunder of the water he heard the high, shrill voice of Dahut, "Father! Take me with you!" He knew at once that she had opened the sea gate.

King Gralon remembered the words of the hermit, "If thy heart offend thee, cut out thy heart and cast it from thee." But he stretched out his hand and pulled his daughter up behind him. He felt her cold arms clinging to him as his horse galloped through the landward gate. And still the sea followed, rising higher and higher.

As he rode, King Gralon looked back over his shoulder. The sea had covered the city. Ys was gone. "My people, I have betrayed you!" cried the king.

When they reached the great cliff that towered above Ys, Dahut's white hand pointed downward. In the black, tormented sea tossing below, the king saw the ghostly

faces of young men who had died for the love of his beautiful daughter. Then he heard behind him the laughter of Dahut.

At that sound, the horse Morwark neighed and reared. With one mighty effort the King freed himself from his daughter's grasp. She fell from the horse, plunged over the edge of the cliff, and vanished into the sea. At once, the waves grew quiet, as if they had found what they sought.

Sick at heart, King Gralon rode away from the lost city of Ys, and made a new capital at Quimper, a city which stands to this day. There, between the towers of the cathedral, is a statue of the king riding his great horse Morwark. The king's ghost still wanders through the villages of Brittany, putting kind and gentle thoughts into the hearts of Breton girls.

As for the Breton fisherman, mending his nets by the fire, on gusty nights when the wind moans, he may hear a knock at the door. When he opens it and finds no one there, he says, "That was not the wind. That was one of Dahut's lovers looking for his home."

And in fine weather, when the sun sparkles on the sea, a sailor, looking down from his little boat into the clear depths of the bay at the Pointe du Raz, may hear the sound of bells and see below him the stone towers of the drowned city of Ys. If it is Easter Day, and if the man is without sin, they say that Ys will rise from the sea before his eyes, with all its sweet bells ringing.

Merlin the Magician

About A.D. 500 there lived a Celtic king named Arthur, who fought against the Saxons. Three hundred years later, his heroic exploits were recorded by the British historian, Nennius. Arthur was a real person, but his name and fame were so great that stories about him became mixed with stories of the old Celtic gods, especially one called Artaios, who was son of the mother goddess, Don (in Ireland, the goddess Dana).

Another four hundred years passed and Geoffrey of Monmouth wrote his own versions of the history of this mythical Arthur, adding stories which had been brought to Brittany by Celtic exiles from Wales. A French poet, Chrestien de Troyes, also working with Breton sources, brought into the saga the characters of Lancelot and Tristan, and the quest for the Holy Grail. By the twelfth and thirteenth centuries, stories of Arthur and his Knights of the Round Table were told all over Europe, because they showed the ideals and aspirations of the age of chivalry.

Beside the glorious figure of Arthur, Merlin the Magician appears as a shadowy, dark presence, but Merlin is connected in myth with a Welsh sun god, Myrddin. In one story Myrddin goes to a Western Island to die as the sun sinks in the Western Sea. A Greek traveler in Britain, writing in the first century, heard of this story and identified it with the Greek myth which told that Cronus, or Chronos (Time), father of Zeus, still lived in the Happy Isles somewhere to the west. In the Welsh myth, Merlin was to return from such a place, the Isle of Avalon, at the time of Arthur's death.

In 1485, William Caxton published Sir Thomas Malory's Morte d'Arthur. *In this, one of the first and greatest*

books ever printed in English, Merlin is almost as im-
portant a figure as the king himself. It is Merlin who knows
all things and who brings to pass the miraculous events
that reveal Arthur as "rightwise king born of all England."

In the ancient days of Britain there lived a Celtic king
named Vortigern. He invited the Saxons to come into his
country to help him in his wars with rival kings. But the
Saxons betrayed Vortigern and drove him into the mountains of northern Wales. There the king's wise men advised him to build a fortress which would withstand any
attack.

Vortigern was pleased with this advice. He traveled
with his wise men from one mountain fastness to another,
searching for the best place to build his castle. At last
they came to Dinas Ffaron, a lofty peak which is now
called Snowden. This mountain commanded all the country round about, and the wise men said, "Build your
fortress here. This place is surely safe from attack."

The king sent for stone masons, carpenters, and builders.
They quarried stone, and hewed down great trees. But
when they began to build the castle, all their work seemed

hopeless. Whatever they raised by day fell down in the night, and the stones and timber disappeared. Again and again the king's workmen tried to build the castle, but each morning their work was gone without a trace.

Vortigern called a council of his wise men and asked them to explain the mystery. They consulted the powers of earth and sky and at last they answered the king, "Your citadel cannot be built without a blood sacrifice. First you must find a boy born without a father. Kill him and sprinkle his blood on the ground where you wish to build."

The king thanked his wise men for their advice and sent messengers to search for a boy who had been born without a father. For a long while they searched in vain.

But at last they arrived at a place now called Caermarthen in Wales. Or perhaps they went as far as Scotland. Some even say the search ended in Brittany. However that may be, one day the messengers came to a field where several boys were playing at ball. One of the boys, a lad with strange bright eyes and long dark hair, threw the ball and called out, "None of you can catch this." And although it looked like an easy throw, not one of the others caught it.

Again and again he threw. The ball seemed to curve in

mid-air, so that no one could catch it. Then the other boys began to taunt the thrower. "You never play fairly, you trickster, you boy without a father."

When the messengers heard this, they knew that they had found the boy they wanted. They seized him and took him to King Vortigern.

"Who is your father?" asked the king.

"I do not know," he answered.

Then the king sent for the mother and demanded to know who was the boy's father.

"I do not know," she said. "No man has ever been my lover. But one night a noble and godlike personage came to me in a dream, and afterward this wonderful boy was born. Whether it was an angel or a beautiful devil who visited me, I know not. But I am sure that this boy's father was no ordinary mortal. Therefore I have called my child Merlin the Magician."

King Vortigern sent the mother away and kept Merlin with him. The next day he assembled his wise men, his soldiers, and all his builders to witness the sacrifice of the boy's life at the place where the castle was to be built.

"Why have you brought me here?" asked Merlin.

"To put you to death," answered Vortigern. "Unless

this ground is sprinkled with your blood, my castle will not stand."

The eyes of Merlin grew dark. "Who told you this?" he asked.

"My wise men," said the king.

"Let me question them," said Merlin. And when the wise men came forward, he said, "If you know that the king's castle will not stand unless my blood is sprinkled on the ground, you must know all things. Tell the king what is hidden under this ground."

But the wise men said, "We do not know."

Merlin said, "There is a pool under this place. Dig and you will find it."

The builders dug and found the pool, as Merlin had said.

"Now tell what is at the bottom of the pool," he commanded the wise men.

But they were confused, and said, "How can we know that?"

Merlin said to the king, "Your wise men do not know, but I do. Search the bottom of the pool and you will find two stone jars joined together."

This was done, and the jars were found. "Now," said

Merlin, "if your wise men are truly wise, they can tell you what is in the jars."

Again the wise men did not know. "Break the jars," Merlin commanded, "and you will find a tent."

This being done, a folded tent appeared. "And what is within the folds of the tent?" Merlin asked the wise men. With shame, they confessed their ignorance.

"There are two dragons within," said Merlin. "Unfold the tent." And when the tent was unfolded, two sleeping dragons were seen, one blood-red, with sun-colored wings, and one white, with talons of bright silver.

"Watch what they do," said Merlin.

The dragons then raised themselves and began to struggle with each other. And all the battles of all the years of the world were like quiet sleep compared with that battle of the two dragons. They flew upward and the valleys echoed with the beating of their wings. Their glorious scales flashed against the sky. Their fiery breath wounded the wind. The lashing of their forked tails cleft mountains asunder so that torrents and waterfalls poured out. On Dinas Ffaron, Vortigern's men were well nigh blinded by the beauty and splendor of the dragons. And as their fighting grew more fierce and furious, the two dragons grew

even stronger and more beautiful, their wings flaming up to heaven, then descending to earth in a halo of golden light. The white dragon drove the red dragon to the western edge of the tent. Then the red one, recovering his strength, fought ever more fiercely until he drove the white dragon eastward, and both disappeared.

"What was the meaning of this omen?" Merlin asked the wise men. And when they again confessed that they did not know, he said to the king, "I will tell you. The pool is a symbol of the world and the tent means your kingdom. The red dragon is the emblem of your people, and the white dragon is that of the Saxons. Even now they hold most of Britain, for the white dragon is stronger than the red one. But the red dragon will forever protect these western mountains. As for you, King Vortigern, depart from Dinas Ffaron, I foresee that you are not meant to build a fortress here."

Then King Vortigern dismissed his foolish wise men, and spared Merlin's life. Merlin came to be known in all the Celtic lands as a great magician. It was he whose magic brought from Ireland to England the giant stones which stand at Stonehenge to this very day.

A hero named Uther went with Merlin on that journey. In time Uther became king, bearing as his emblem a silken banner emblazoned with the red dragon, so that he was called Uther Pendragon. He fought valiantly to subdue and unite all the warring kings of Britain under the dragon banner, but this he could never do. When Merlin saw that the struggle would be longer than the life of Uther Pendragon, he found for him a wife, the fair Igraine. She was a young widow whose husband had been slain by Uther in battle and she had her castle at Tintagel on the coast of Cornwall. There Uther wooed her, and some say that Arthur, son of Uther Pendragon, was born at Tintagel.

Soon afterward, Merlin came to the king and said, "Sir, I foresee that you have not long to live. You must give your son to me. Until he is grown to manhood I will keep him in hiding, safe from your enemies, who would kill him if they could. Bring him to me tonight at the postern gate of this castle."

Under cover of darkness, as Merlin commanded, the child was brought to him, wrapped in rich cloth of gold. Then Merlin carried him away and gave him into the care of a worthy knight, Sir Ector. This good man did not know that the child was the son of Uther Pendragon, but he loved Arthur like a father, and Sir Ector's wife nursed the baby as if he had been her own child.

Within two years, Uther Pendragon won a great victory over his enemies, but as Merlin had foretold, the king soon fell sick unto death. Then Merlin said to him, "Call all your barons and noblemen together."

When this was done, Merlin stood before them and called aloud to King Uther so that all could hear, "Sir, shall your son Arthur be king after you?"

And Uther said in the hearing of all, "I give him God's blessing and mine, and I bid him to claim the crown." With these words, the king died.

Arthur grew to be a man in the household of Sir Ector. He knew no other father, and he loved Sir Ector's son, Kay, like a brother. During these years the kingdom was in danger, for in spite of the king's last words, every lord and baron wished to seize the throne. At last, when the time was ripe, Merlin called all of them to London and told them that God would work a miracle to show who should be king. A throng of great men came to London and went into church to pray, for it was Christmastide. When they came out again, they saw in the churchyard a great square stone. On the stone stood an anvil of steel a foot high, and thrust through it into the stone they saw the blade of a fair sword, inscribed with letters of gold: WHOSO PULLETH OUT THIS SWORD OF THIS STONE AND ANVIL IS RIGHT-WISE KING BORN OF ALL ENGLAND.

Then some of the lords, who wanted to be king, tried to pull the sword from the stone, but none could move it. While they were still waiting for the sign from God which Merlin had promised, New Year's Day came, and it was decided to hold a tournament.

Now Kay had been newly knighted and he wanted to prove his valor in the tournament. But when he came to the field where the lists had been set up, he found that he had forgotten his sword. He asked Arthur to ride back to his father's lodging and bring his sword to him. Arthur rode back with a good will, and as he passed the churchyard, he saw the sword in the stone. When he came to Sir Ector's house the door was locked, for all had gone to the jousting. Then Arthur said to himself, "I will ride to the churchyard and take that sword from the stone, for my brother Kay must have a sword."

When he came to the churchyard, he dismounted and tied his horse to the stile. He took the sword by the hilt, and lightly and fiercely pulled it out of the stone. Then he rode back to Sir Kay, and gave him the sword. As soon as Kay saw it, he knew that it was the sword of the stone and he rode with it to his father and said, "Sir, here is the sword of the stone. Therefore I must be king of this land."

But when Sir Ector saw the sword, he made Arthur and Kay return with him to the church, and he made Kay swear an oath to tell truly how he came by the sword. "Sir," said Sir Kay, "I got it from my brother Arthur, who brought it to me."

"How did you get this sword?" Sir Ector said to Arthur.

"Sir, I will tell you," said Arthur. "When I went home for my brother's sword, I found the door locked and nobody there. So I came here and pulled the sword out of the stone."

"Did any knight see you do this?" asked Sir Ector.

"No," said Arthur.

Then Sir Ector said to Arthur, "Now I understand that you must be king of this land, for none can be king but he who draws out this sword. Let me see whether you can put the sword as it was and pull it out again."

"That is not difficult," said Arthur, and he put the sword into the stone again.

Then Sir Ector tried to pull out the sword and failed. Sir Kay pulled at the sword with all his might, but it would not move.

"Now you shall try again," Sir Ector said to Arthur.

"I will," said Arthur, and pulled it out easily. Then Sir Ector and Sir Kay knelt before him.

"Alas," said Arthur, "my own dear father and brother, why do you kneel to me?"

"I never was your father, my lord Arthur," said Sir Ector. "Now I know that you are of nobler blood than I." Then he told Arthur how he had cared for him by Merlin's command.

Arthur made great lament when he understood that Sir Ector was not his father. "To you and your wife, my good lady and mother, I owe more than to anyone in the world," he said. "If by God's will I ever become king, ask of me what you will, and I shall not fail you."

Sir Ector said, "I ask only that Sir Kay, your foster brother, be steward of all your lands."

"That shall be done," said Arthur.

Then they went to the archbishop and told him how Arthur had won the sword. And on the twelfth day of Christmas he pulled it from the stone again, while all the barons looked on. Many great lords were angry and said it was a shame that the realm should be governed by a beardless boy of humble birth. So at Candlemas many more great lords came to try for the sword, but none could pull it from the stone. Still they would not acknowledge Arthur as king and said that all must try again at Easter. Once again at Easter, Arthur alone pulled out the sword. Yet some of the great lords delayed his coronation until Pentecost.

At Pentecost all manner of men were allowed to try the sword, and none could prevail. But Arthur pulled it out before all the lords and all the common people who were there. And the common people cried, "We will have Arthur for our king with no more delay. It is God's will that he shall be our king and we will slay anyone who stands against him."

Then rich and poor knelt down and begged Arthur's forgiveness because they had delayed so long.

Arthur took the sword in both his hands and offered it upon the church altar and was made a knight. Soon afterward, he was crowned. He swore that he would be a true king and would stand for justice all the days of his life. And he righted wrongs that had been done since the death of Uther Pendragon.

Some say that Arthur ruled his kingdom from Caerleon in Wales. Others say that his castle was in the south of England near Merlin's magic circle of Stonehenge. However that may be, Arthur's capital came to be known as Camelot, and when he had been crowned, other kings with their hundreds of knights gathered there. Arthur sent them presents, but they said that they would take no presents from a beardless boy of low blood. Then Merlin came among them by magic and they asked him, "Why is that boy Arthur made your king?"

"Sirs," said Merlin, "he is Uther Pendragon's son, and whatever you say, he will be king, and will overcome all his enemies. Before he dies, he shall be king of all England, Wales, Ireland, and Scotland, and more realms than these." Then he vanished from their midst.

Merlin told Arthur to go out and speak to those proud kings, but when he went, they gave him hard words. Some of them prepared to lay siege to his castle, but many of the best men that were with the kings came to his side, and that comforted him.

"Sir," said Merlin to Arthur, "do not fight with the sword that you got by miracle until you must. Then draw it out and do your best."

And when the kings attacked Arthur's castle from all sides, he drew his sword and went out to meet them. His sword was so bright in his enemies' eyes that it gave light like thirty torches. And the common people arose to help him with clubs and staves, until all the kings and knights who were left alive fled and departed. Merlin advised Arthur to let them go.

By magic, Merlin had made for Uther Pendragon the Round Table that became the glory of Arthur's reign. Around that table Arthur gathered the best knights in the realm. And always Merlin stood at the king's right hand, warning of danger, foretelling the future with wisdom beyond that of mortal man, and weaving spells from his book of enchantment.

But at last Merlin grew old, and with an old man's folly he fell in love with a fair young witch, the Lady of the Lake. She begged him to tell her a spell for sleeping, and when he gave her the secret, she put him to sleep and imprisoned him with another spell. She stole his magic book, which was lost forever.

It may be that Merlin's prison is a house of glass, or a bush of whitethorn laden with bloom. Perhaps he sleeps surrounded by perpetual mist on some mountain of Wales, at Stonehenge, or as the ancient books say, he may rest in "a close neither of iron nor steel nor timber nor of stone, but of the air without any other thing, by enchantment so strong that it may never be undone while the world endures." No man knows where Merlin sleeps.

How Gareth of Orkney
Won His Spurs

The Orkney Islands lie north of Scotland in a grim
and restless sea. In the Orkneys there are still fairy
raths dating back to prehistoric Celtic days, and
there are "Standing Stones" like those at Stonehenge. Gareth's great size may reflect the physical
traits of Norsemen who had settled in the Orkneys.

King Lot of Orkney was one of the rebel lords
who refused to acknowledge Arthur as king. His

wife, Morgause, King Arthur's half sister by the fair Igraine, became the mother of Mordred, who was to destroy Arthur's court. Gareth was the youngest son of Morgause, who, like many mothers in myth and in real life, was unwilling to let him go from her.

Gareth was determined to be a Knight of the Round Table. This mystical table was made by Merlin and given as a wedding present to Arthur from Guinevere's father. It had once been owned by Uther Pendragon and symbolized the roundness of the world as well as the ideal of equality for all of Arthur's knights.

The last of the adversaries met by Gareth in this story is the Red Knight of the Red Plain. Gareth is advised to fight him after the noon hour because, like a sun god, the Red Knight's strength grows until midday, then wanes. But the chief mythical significance of the adventure which Gareth undertakes lies in the quest to rescue the Lady Lyonnesse of the Castle Perilous. This concerns the journey which the mythical hero must make along a road of trials toward his dream of a full and perfect life. The beautiful, faraway princess symbolizes this life. She is difficult to attain, but that is the very quality which makes her all the more desirable. Winning her is the final test *of the hero, and in myth the simplehearted and gentle man is the most likely of all heroes to succeed in the quest.*

The story of Gareth begins with sunny good humor, but his life had a tragic ending. Gareth had admired Lancelot more than any other Knight of the Round Table, and begged to be knighted by him. After the love affair between Lancelot and Guinevere, Gareth was accidentally killed by Lancelot, who came to rescue the queen from being burned at the stake.

Each year, when the Round Table was in its glory, King Arthur liked to hear of some great adventure before he sat down at the high feast of Pentecost. Once, when he was waiting to keep the feast at a seaside castle in Wales, Sir Gawain looked from a window and saw in the courtyard a tall young man on horseback, followed by a dwarf. The young man dismounted and the dwarf led the horse away.

Gawain said to the king, "Sir, you can begin the feast, for here comes an adventurer." So Arthur sat at the table with all his knights around him.

Then there came into the hall the goodliest and fairest

young man that ever they had seen. He was big, broad in the shoulders, and handsome. His manner was friendly, modest, and mild. Arthur made him welcome to the feast.

"God bless you, King Arthur," said the young stranger, "and God bless the fellowship of the Table Round. I have come to ask you for three favors. Today I ask for the first. It is a favor you can easily grant."

"Granted before you ask," said Arthur.

"Then give me meat and drink for one year. At the end of the year I will ask my other two favors."

"This is nothing. Ask something better," said Arthur, "for my heart tells me that you will prove to be a man of great worth. What is your name?"

"I cannot tell you," said the youth.

"A goodly young man like you does not know his own name?" said the king in jest. Then he told Sir Kay, his steward, to give the youth the best of meat and drink and all things befitting a lord's son.

"There is no need for that expense," Sir Kay said to himself. "The fellow is clearly a peasant, asking for meat and drink. A gentleman would have asked for a horse and armor. And since he has no name, I shall call him Beaumains, Fair Hands, for he has the biggest hands I have ever seen. He can work and eat in the kitchen. At the end of a year he will be fat as a hog, as peasants like to be."

Now Sir Gawain felt a special kinship with the youth, as well he might, though he did not yet know why. And Sir Lancelot was kind because of his own great gentleness and courtesy. Both were angry with Sir Kay when they saw how he scorned and mocked "Beaumains." Both offered to feed the young man with their own followers. But Beaumains refused their offers, saying that the king had put him under the care of Sir Kay. He took his place among the kitchen boys and shared their work without complaint. But in their free time the kitchen boys competed in feats of strength and Beaumains always won. When there were joustings and tournaments, he was always watching.

A year passed and the king went to Caerleon for Pentecost. Once again he wished to hear of some adventure before he sat down at the feast. Then came a squire who said to the king, "Sir, you may sit down to eat, for here comes a damsel with a strange adventure to tell."

At once, a proud damsel came into the hall and said,

"Sir, I have come to you because I have heard that your knights are the noblest in the world. I ask help from one of them for a great lady who is held prisoner in her castle."

"What is her name?" asked the king. "And where does she dwell?"

"I will not give her name or tell you where she dwells," said the damsel. "But the tyrant who holds her there and destroys her lands is called Sir Ironside, the Red Knight of the Red Plain, and he is an evil man."

"I know him," said Sir Gawain. "He is evil indeed, and he has the strength of seven men. Once I myself barely escaped from him with my life."

"Fair damsel," said King Arthur, "I cannot send one of my knights on this perilous adventure unless you will tell me who the lady is and where she dwells."

Then Beaumains stepped forward and knelt before the king. "Sir," he said, "I have been for twelve months in your kitchen and have had my meat and drink as you promised. Now I will ask my last favors. The first is, to let me have this adventure. And last of all, let Sir Lancelot ride after me. If I win my spurs, let him make me a knight."

The king was well pleased. "All this shall be done," he said.

But the damsel cried, "For shame! Must I have a kitchen boy for my champion?" And she took her horse and rode off.

At that moment there came into the courtyard the same dwarf who had arrived with Beaumains a year before. He was leading a fine horse which carried on its back a breast-plate and a sword. Beaumains took leave of the king and asked Sir Lancelot to follow with all speed. Then he took the sword and armor, mounted the horse, and without shield or lance, rode after the damsel. The dwarf ran be-hind.

As Beaumains overtook the damsel, Sir Kay came after him and ordered him to stop, for he thought Beaumains unworthy to be the champion of so proud a lady. Beau-mains rode on.

Sir Kay called angrily, "Fellow, do you not know my voice?"

Beaumains turned his horse and answered, "I know you for the most ungentle knight of King Arthur's court." Then Kay put his spear in the saddle rest and ran straight upon him, and Beaumains came fast upon Kay with his sword in his hand. He thrust Kay's spear aside and struck such a blow that Kay fell from his horse and lay stunned on the ground. Beaumains took Sir Kay's spear and shield. He put the dwarf on Kay's horse, mounted his own, and rode on after the damsel.

Now Sir Lancelot and his squires had caught up with Beaumains and had seen the whole adventure. "Will you too joust with me, Sir Lancelot?" asked Beaumains in all courtesy.

"Willingly," said Lancelot. And they fought as worthy champions fight, first on horse and then on foot. Lancelot marveled at the strength of the young man, for he fought skillfully and tirelessly, more like a giant than like a man. At last Lancelot said, "Beaumains, you need not fight so sore. We have no quarrel."

"That is true," said Beaumains, "but it does me good to feel your might. And yet, my lord, I did not use all my strength. Do you think that I shall some day be worthy of knighthood?"

"You are worthy this day," said Lancelot. "I will knight you here and now. But first tell me your name and family."

"I will tell you. I am Gareth of Orkney, youngest brother of Sir Gawain, though he had never seen me until I came to King Arthur's court. I am nephew to the king. Promise to tell no one until I have truly won my spurs."

Then Lancelot dubbed Gareth of Orkney a knight and returned to Arthur's court, but his squires had to carry Sir Kay on a shield. Never again would Sir Kay be scornful of a young man only because he would not tell his name or say why he came to court.

Sir Gareth rode on and overtook the proud damsel. "Is it you again, Beaumains?" she said. "You smell of the kitchen and your clothes are foul with kitchen grease under your armor. Do you think I like you better for wounding that knight? You did not fight fairly. Go away, you lubber, you turner of spits and washer of ladles."

"Madam," said Gareth, "say what you will, I shall fight against any knight who bars your way. I have sworn to King Arthur to follow this adventure to the end, or die in the attempt."

"You would not face the Red Knight of the Red Plain for all the soup in the kitchen," said she.

"I will try," he said.

As they rode on, they came to a woods and saw a man riding toward them at full speed. "Help me!" he cried. "My lord has been attacked by six robbers, and I fear they will kill him."

"Take me to him," said Gareth. He set spurs to his

horse and followed the man to where a knight lay bound hand and foot, surrounded by the six robbers. Gareth slew three of the robbers, and when the others turned and fled, he went after them and slew them also. Then he freed the knight from his bonds. The knight thanked him and bade him ride with the lady to his castle, where he might reward Gareth for his brave deeds.

"Sir," said Gareth, "I have had enough reward. Today I was made a knight by noble Sir Lancelot."

But the damsel, unknowing, rode toward the knight's castle with her head held high. "Do you think you have pleased me, Beaumains?" she said to Gareth. "You still smell of the kitchen. You have had good fortune, that is all. Wait until you meet the Red Knight."

When they reached the castle of the knight whom Gareth had rescued, he offered them good cheer and set a table for Gareth and the damsel. But she said, "Beaumains is more fit for pig-sticking than for sitting with a damsel of high degree." The knight was ashamed of her words. He took Gareth to another table and ate there with him, leaving the proud damsel to sit by herself.

The next day Gareth rode on with that lady until evening, and she never gave him a civil word.

They came to a black field and saw a black hawthorn tree with a black banner and a black shield hanging on it. Beside the tree stood a great black horse covered with trappings of black silk. And on the horse sat a knight in black armor.

"Damsel," said he, "have you brought this knight of King Arthur to be your champion against me?"

"No," she said, "he is only a kitchen boy, and I would gladly be rid of him."

"Then I will take his horse and armor from him," said the knight in black armor. "It would be a shame to do more harm than that to a kitchen boy."

"I am a gentleman born," said Gareth, "and I am about to cross your field. Let us see if you can take my horse and armor." Then they rode against each other and came together with a sound like thunder. The knight in black armor smote Gareth with many strokes and hurt him full sore, but Gareth fought him to the death. He took the black horse and the black armor and rode after the damsel.

"Away, kitchen boy, out of the wind," she said. "The smell of your clothes offends me. Alas, that such a knave as you should slay so good a knight, and all by luck. But the Red Knight will kill you. Away, flee while you can."

"Damsel," said Gareth, "you are not courteous to rebuke me as you do, for I think I have done you good service. Always you say that I shall be beaten by knights that we meet, but for all that, they lie in the dust. Rebuke me no more."

Then they came to a city rich and fair, and between them and the city a meadow, new mown and full of blue pavilions. The damsel said, "Beaumains, the noble lord who owns that city comes in fair weather with five hundred knights to joust in his meadow. You had better flee before he sets upon you with all his knights."

"If he is noble, he will not set upon me with five hundred knights," said Gareth. "And if they come one at a time, I will face them as long as I live."

Then the damsel said, "I pray you, save yourself while you can. You and your horse have fought long and hard and my lady's castle lies not far off. There you will have the hardest fight of all."

Gareth answered, "Be that as it may, I shall have dealt with this knight two hours after noon. We shall come to your lady's castle while it is still daylight."

"What manner of man are you!" said the damsel.

"Never did a woman treat a knight so shamefully as I have you, and you have always answered me courteously. Only a man of gentle blood would do so."

Gareth answered, "I ate my meat in King Arthur's kitchen so that I might know who are my true friends. I never minded your words, for the more you angered me, the better I fought. Whether I am a gentleman born or not, I have done you gentleman's service, and I will do better yet, before I leave you."

"Alas," she said, "forgive me."

"With all my heart," said Gareth. "And now that we are friends, I think there is no knight living but I am strong enough to face him."

Then the knight of the blue pavilions came against Gareth clad all in blue armor, and Gareth rode against him with such force that their spears broke in pieces and their horses fell to the earth. But the two knights sprang from their horses. They raised their shields and drew their swords and gave many great strokes. Thus they fought two hours and more until their shields and their armor were hewn to bits and in many places they were wounded. At the last, Sir Gareth gave such a blow that the blue knight begged for mercy, saying, "You shall have homage and fealty of me, and my hundred knights shall be always at your command."

He made Sir Gareth and the damsel welcome in his pavilion and he asked where they were going. Sir Gareth said that he would fight against the Red Knight of the Red Plain to relieve the siege of a fair lady's castle.

The blue knight answered, "The Knight of the Red Plain is the most perilous knight now living. He has long wished to do battle with some valiant knight of King Arthur's Round Table, even Sir Lancelot or Sir Gawain, to prove his strength against them." And he asked the damsel, "Are you not sister to the lady who is besieged by the Red Knight? Is not your name Lynette?"

"It is," said she, "and I am indeed the sister of that unfortunate lady, Lyonnesse, who is besieged in the Castle Perilous."

Then the knight of the blue pavilions pledged to Sir Gareth the homage and fealty of himself and his hundred knights, and Sir Gareth rode on with the Lady Lynette until they came close to the Castle Perilous. They heard great noise of battle and they passed tall elm trees where hung the bodies of forty knights in armor. From the branch of a sycamore tree nearby hung a great ivory horn.

"Fair sir," said Lynette, "if any knight blows this horn, the Red Knight will come to do battle with him. But do not blow the horn before midday, for the Red Knight's strength increases until high noon. All these knights came here to rescue my sister, the Lady Lyonnesse, and the Red Knight overcame them and put them to this shameful death."

"I will fight him at his strongest," said Sir Gareth, and he blew the horn so eagerly that the Castle Perilous rang with the sound and the Lady Lyonnesse and all within the castle looked over the walls and out the windows. The Red Knight of the Red Plain armed himself, and all was blood-red—his armor, spear, and shield. Then he rode to a little vale close by the castle that all within and without might behold the battle.

"Yonder is my sister, the Lady Lyonnesse," said Lynette, and pointed to a far window.

Sir Gareth said, "Even from afar, she seems a fair lady. I will gladly do battle for her." Then he raised his hand to her and in her far window he saw the lady raise her hand to him.

But the Red Knight called to Sir Gareth, "Look not at

her but at me. She is my lady and I have fought many battles for her."

"I think it was a waste of labor," said Gareth. "To love one who does not love you is great folly. I will rescue her or die in the attempt."

"Do you say so?" answered the Red Knight. "Take warning by the knights that you saw hang on yonder elm trees."

But Sir Gareth said, "That shameful sight only gives me more courage to fight against you."

"Talk no longer with me," said the Red Knight. "Make yourself ready."

Then they put their spears in their rests and came together with all the might they had. They smote each other in the midst of their shields so that their breastplates burst. Both knights fell to the ground with such force that all within the castle thought their necks had been broken. But they rose and put their shields before them, and drew their swords and ran together like two fierce lions. Each gave the other a blow upon his helmet, so that both reeled back. Again they recovered and fought until great pieces were hewn from their armor and their shields.

So they battled till it was past noon. Again and again

they came face to face, locked in struggle, panting and bleeding. Thus they endured until evening. Their armor was so far hewn that they fought half naked. Now and again they sat down to rest and their pages unlaced their helmets. When Sir Gareth's helmet was off, he looked at the distant window, and the faraway face of the Lady Lyonnesse made his heart light and joyful.

At last the Red Knight smote Gareth so that his sword fell out of his hand. Another blow on the helmet drove Gareth to the ground, and the Red Knight fell upon him to hold him down.

Then Lynette cried out, "Beaumains, what has become of your courage? My sister is watching you."

When Gareth heard that, he threw off his enemy, picked up his sword, and leaped to his feet. He struck the sword from the Red Knight's hand and smote him on the helmet so that he dropped to the earth. Then Gareth fell upon him and unlaced his helmet to slay him. The Red Knight asked for mercy.

Gareth said, "How can you ask for your life when you caused so many knights to die shameful deaths?"

"Sir," said the Red Knight, "once I loved a lady whose brother was slain. She said that Sir Lancelot or Sir Gawain

had killed him, and she made me swear to kill every knight
I met until I killed those two knights."

Then many earls and barons and noble knights came to
Sir Gareth and begged him to spare the life of the Red
Knight. "For," said they, "his death will not help you,
and his misdeeds cannot be undone. Therefore, let him
make amends to all, and we will swear homage and fealty
to you."

"Fair lords," said Gareth, "I will release him. But let
him yield himself to the lady of the castle and let him make
amends first of all to her."

"This I will do," said the Red Knight, and he went to
the castle to ask forgiveness of the Lady Lyonnesse. She
received him kindly. But when Gareth went to the castle,
she sent a message to the portal, saying, "Go your way,
Sir Knight, until I know more of you. Until then, trust
me, I shall be true to you."

Then secretly she told her brother to follow Gareth and
to capture the dwarf who was always with him. She would
come to the castle of her brother, and there she would
question the dwarf.

Sir Gareth rode away very sorrowfully. He rode here
and there, and knew not where he rode, until it was dark

night. He could not sleep for love of the lady of the Castle Perilous. The next night, weary and sick at heart, he gave his horse into the care of the dwarf and lay down to rest with his head on his shield.

And while Gareth slept, the brother of the Lady Lyonnesse came softly behind the dwarf. He picked him up and rode away with him as fast as ever he might toward his own castle. But the dwarf cried out to Sir Gareth for help. And Sir Gareth awoke and followed them through marshes and fields until he lost sight of them. Many times his horse plunged over his head into deep mire, for he did not know his way. And while Sir Gareth was painfully making his way to the castle, the dwarf had told the Lady Lyonnesse that her unknown champion was nephew to King Arthur and that his name was Sir Gareth of Orkney.

When at last Sir Gareth came to the gate with angry face and drawn sword and demanded his dwarf, the Lady Lyonnesse said to her brother, "I would speak with Sir Gareth, but he must not know who I am."

Then her brother let down the drawbridge and opened the gate and said, "Sir, I will return your dwarf to you and I beg your forgiveness. I pray you to enter and take such cheer as I can give, for your dwarf has told me who you are and what noble deeds you have done."

Sir Gareth's anger was appeased. He dismounted and his dwarf came to take the horse. "Oh, little fellow," said Sir Gareth, "I have had many evil adventures for your sake."

Then he went into the great hall and he saw the Lady Lyonnesse disguised as a strange princess. They exchanged many fair words and kind looks. And Sir Gareth thought to himself, "Would to God that the faraway lady of the Castle Perilous were as fair as this lady!"

They danced together. And the more Sir Gareth beheld the lady, the more he loved her. He burned with such love that he was out of his wits. And when they went to supper, he could not eat, for his love was so hot that he did not know where he was.

And the Lady Lyonnesse said to her brother, "Now I know that I would rather Sir Gareth were mine to have and to hold as my husband than any king or prince in this world, and if I may not have him, I will have none. He is my first love, and he shall be the last."

Her brother went to Sir Gareth and said, "Sir, good cheer. She loves you as well as you love her, and better, if better may be."

"If I can believe that," said Sir Gareth, "there is no

happier man alive than I will be."

Then the noble knight Sir Gareth went to the Lady Lyonnesse and kissed her many times. And she told him that she was the same lady he had done battle for, the lady of the Castle Perilous. And she told him how she had caused her brother to take away his dwarf, "to know certainly who you were and whence you came."

Then there came in Lynette, the damsel who had ridden with him many dreary ways, and Sir Gareth was even more glad than before. And he and the Lady Lyonnesse plighted their troth to love, and never to fail while their life lasted.

Thus ends the tale of Sir Gareth of Orkney that wedded the Lady Lyonnesse of the Castle Perilous.

The Last Battle

Most of the ancient Celtic gods and heroes appear in the Arthurian cycle of stories, though in disguise. Arthur is the son of the mother goddess, Don. Gawain and Mordred, nephews or sons of Arthur, represent gods of light and of darkness. They are good and evil, battling to the end. In Welsh mythology, Bedwyr is a god unequaled in swiftness. He has only one arm, but he can overcome nine adversaries. Later Bedwyr becomes Sir Bedivere. Excalibur is the Latinized name for a fairy sword which in an Irish story is wielded by the hero Fergus. Like the Scottish Lad of Luck in this collection, Fergus uses his sword to slay a lake monster. When he knows that he himself must die, Fergus asks that his sword be given only to another hero of the same name, so that, as with Excalibur, "for all time, men shall rehearse the story of the sword."

Geoffrey of Monmouth said that Excalibur had been forged in "the Isle of Avalon." Glastonbury, an ancient Celtic settlement in southwest England, was once an island called Avalon. There, in a wide green stretch of lawn, rise the broken arches of an abbey where, hundreds of years ago, two graves were found. Under one of the stones was a leaden cross incised with the words: HIC IACET SEPULTUS INCLYTUS REX ARTHURUS IN INSULA AVALONIA. "Here lies buried the renowned King Arthur in the Isle of Avalon."

But people who live near the sea, as did the Celts, have always told of a Happy Isle to the west, where the sun sets. Morgan le Fay, one of the three queens who came to take Arthur to Avalon, was a sea and island goddess,

known in Jreland as Mor, wife of the sea god Lir. Dahut,
in the story "The Bells of Ys," is very like Morgan le Fay,
and the Jle de Sein, off the coast of Brittany, had some of
the mystic aura of Avalon. Wherever the Happy Jsle may
be, the hero departs for it at the end of his life, unafraid.
He may not have been without sin, but he has battled
against evil to the last, and in Avalon he is only sleeping.
He will come again when his people need him.

Many times in his glorious reign King Arthur drew a sword
in deeds of valor and chivalry to rescue the weak and
help the needy. One of his swords he got by a miracle
before he was crowned. This was the sword of the stone.
The other was Excalibur, a sword of beauty and power
which he got from the Lady of the Lake, whom Merlin
loved. But in spite of Arthur's swords and in spite of
Arthur's valor, the end came for him, as it must come to
all men. It happened in this wise.

The Holy Grail appeared in England, and many Knights
of the Round Table rode away to try if they might be
found worthy to see that gracious Cup from which Our

Lord drank at the Last Supper. And one, Galahad, who was without fear and without reproach, did indeed behold the Grail.

But after the Holy Grail had disappeared again from the earth, others seeking the Cup were lost in fogs and fens, following a will-o'-the-wisp to their death. And of those who returned after long wanderings, some began to doubt among themselves who was true to the king, and who was false, through coldness of heart or ambition for the throne. The Knights of the Round Table no longer fought for the glory of the court and the common good of all, for they saw that King Arthur was growing old.

Now in the king's old age, his queen, Guinevere, fell in love with Lancelot, so that a bitter conflict arose. Some of the knights followed the king, and some followed Lancelot. In the bitter fighting, Lancelot killed Gaheris and Gareth, the brothers of Sir Gawain. And Gawain was sorely grieved by their deaths. He told the king that Lancelot was a traitor, so that Lancelot was banished from the court. Sir Lancelot would not fight against his liege lord, King Arthur, but withdrew across the sea to his own castle in France.

When Lancelot had gone, Sir Gawain said to King Arthur, "Follow him, my lord, and attack him!"

But King Arthur said, "Many a time he has rescued me and you, both on horseback and on foot."

"Nay," Sir Gawain answered, "we are past that at this time. He is false to you and to me." At last he persuaded the king.

Arthur was full of years and his heart was heavy with care, but he made a great host ready. He called his nephew, Sir Mordred, to be chief ruler of all England, for Sir Mordred was brother to Sir Gawain. And Mordred was very pleased.

Then King Arthur and Sir Gawain departed from England with a great army. It was a multitude that sailed across the narrow sea and landed with the king on the coast of France. They rode over hill and valley with armor shining and with banners streaming in the wind, until they came to a great plain where lay the castle of Sir Lancelot.

Even within the castle walls, Sir Lancelot heard the distant thunder of trampling war horses. Hastening to the battlements, he looked out and saw the army coming in a cloud of dust. In the forefront he saw his once-loved friend,

Sir Gawain, riding at the side of King Arthur. And the army advanced until it stood at the very foot of the castle walls, and encamped there, besieging the castle.

Then Lancelot said, "Peace is better than war. I shall send a messenger to my lord Arthur to ask for a treaty." Arthur would have granted the treaty, but Sir Gawain would not, and Arthur heeded the words of Gawain.

So there was much cruel and bitter fighting, and many on both sides lost their lives. Sir Lancelot did not fight willingly against his old companions of the Round Table, but remained within the castle and sent others out to fight in his stead.

Sir Gawain, bent on avenging the death of his brothers, rode every day on his great war horse up and down in front of the gates, shouting insults, provoking Lancelot, and taunting him for his want of courage and honor, until Sir Lancelot knew that a battle against his friend must come. On a fateful day the drawbridge fell, and he rode out to face Sir Gawain.

Now listen to a dolorous adventure. Three times these gallant knights charged fiercely against each other and neither could gain the victory. Then with a mighty thrust Sir Lancelot's sword sheared through the armor of Sir

Gawain and through his shoulder and his chest, and Sir Gawain fell to the ground. Sir Lancelot rode back to his castle very sorrowfully, and the gates closed behind him.

Sir Gawain lay sick near a month. Before his wounds could heal, there came from England evil tidings that Mordred had seized the throne and crown of Britain to keep them for himself. So Arthur withdrew his army from France and returned in haste to England with his great fleet of ships and galleys.

When they came close to the cliffs of Dover, there they saw Mordred with his army drawn up on the beach. Then there was launching of great boats and small and much slaughter of knights and noble men. But King Arthur leaped into the shallow water and fought his way to land so bravely that no man might prevent him, and his knights fiercely followed him, until Sir Mordred fled with all his people.

When this battle was done, then was Sir Gawain found in a great boat, lying half dead. And the king, kneeling down, took Sir Gawain in his arms. "Alas," he said, "in Lancelot and you I most had my joy. Now I have lost you both."

"My death day is come," said Gawain, "and all through

my own folly. I am smitten upon the old wound which Lancelot gave me. Had he been with you as he once was, this unhappy war had never begun, for his strength held your enemies at bay. Give me paper, pen, and ink, and I will beg him to return." Then he wrote to Sir Lancelot, "This day I was hurt to the death in the same wound that you gave me. Now for all the love that ever was between us, come over the sea in all haste and rescue the noble king that made you a knight, for Sir Mordred has betrayed him." And Sir Gawain yielded up the spirit.

"My quarrel cannot wait for Lancelot," said Arthur. Then he pursued Sir Mordred to the west and they fought again, and the army of King Arthur was victorious. But many noble knights were slain. Again Mordred withdrew, and again he assembled his army, and King Arthur pursued him.

But as the king lay asleep in his tent on the battlefield at night, he dreamed a dream, and he saw Sir Gawain, who was dead. Sir Gawain said to the king in his dream, "Sir, God has given me leave to warn you, for if you fight tomorrow with Sir Mordred, you will be slain and your army with you. Do not do battle but make a treaty until Sir Lancelot and all his noble knights shall come to rescue you with honor." Then the figure of Sir Gawain disappeared.

The king called his knights around him and told them of his vision, and they agreed to make a treaty with Mordred.

King Arthur and Sir Mordred vowed to meet in a certain field between the two armies. The place was in a valley near a lake that opened on the Western Sea. And the two armies were drawn up, facing each other.

King Arthur chose six knights to come with him, and Sir Mordred chose six knights. It was agreed that none should draw a sword. Arthur and Mordred came to sign the treaty, and when wine was fetched, they drank together. But it chanced that a snake lay under a bush nearby. And the snake uncoiled itself and slid through the dust and raised its head to strike. One of the knights of Sir Mordred saw the snake and drew his sword to slay it. And when the armies saw that sword drawn, they blew trumpets and shouted grimly, and rushed to battle with fury. So began the last great battle of the west.

Thus they fought all the day long till it was near night and a hundred thousand lay dead upon the field. In the fall of darkness the king looked about him and cried out in grief, for of all his knights, only one, Sir Bedivere, remained alive, and he was sore wounded. "Now," said Arthur, "I am come to my end and all my court of knighthood with me. Would to God that I could find the traitor."

Then he saw Mordred standing alone, leaning upon his sword among the slain.

"Give me my spear," said Arthur. "There is the man who has worked all this woe."

Sir Bedivere answered, "Sir, let him be. Come what may, he is doomed. If you live, that will be your revenge. Remember what the spirit of Sir Gawain told you in your dream. This unlucky day is past. Let well enough alone."

But the king said, "I shall never have a better chance to kill him. Tide me life, tide me death, he shall not escape me." Then he took his spear in both hands and ran toward Sir Mordred, crying, "Traitor, have at thee."

Mordred heard the king and ran forward with his sword in his hand. Then King Arthur leveled the spear and drove it with great strength through the body of his enemy. Sir Mordred did not fall but still advanced, thrusting his body forward until the spear stood out an arm's length behind him. Still he came on with his sword held in both hands, smiting Arthur on the side of the head so that he pierced deep through the king's helmet. Then Sir Mordred fell dead to the earth.

Arthur too fell to the earth, fainting. Sir Bedivere lifted him and the king said, "Sir, this is my death wound. Take me hence."

Sir Bedivere saw a ruined chapel with a broken cross upon the field of battle, not far from the water side, and there he led the king. Now while Arthur lay in the chapel, Sir Bedivere heard the sound of people shouting on the field, and from the doorway he saw by the moonlight that robbers were pillaging and looting, taking rings and jewels from the bodies of many noble knights, and killing the wounded for their riches. When Sir Bedivere saw it, he would have taken the king to some town for safety, but King Arthur said, "I cannot stand. My time has come. Therefore, take Excalibur, my good sword. Go with it to the lake and throw it into the water. Come quickly back and tell me what you have seen."

Sir Bedivere took the sword and left the chapel. Then in the moonlight the golden hilt studded with jewels flashed and blazed in his hand, and he said to himself, "If I throw away this rich sword, no good will come of it, but only loss." And he hid Excalibur under a tree. Then he came again to the king and said that he had thrown the sword into the water.

The king said, "What did you see?"

"Sir," he answered, "I saw nothing but waves and winds."

"You do not speak the truth," said Arthur. "Go and do my command, if you love me. Throw away the sword."

Sir Bedivere went again, and again when he looked at Excalibur, he thought it sin and shame to throw away that noble sword. So he returned and told the king that he had done his command.

"What did you see?" said the king.

"Sir," he answered, "I saw nothing but the waves breaking on the shore. The tide is going out."

Then Arthur cried, "You have betrayed me twice. You are untrue. Go quickly and obey me, for your long delay puts me in danger of my life. Who would believe that you, whom I made a knight, would see me dead for the sake of a jeweled sword?"

Sir Bedivere ran from the chapel to the tree where he had hidden the sword. Swiftly he took it up and went to the lake shore. There he bound the belt about the hilt and threw the sword as far as he might into the water. Then from the lake there rose a hand and an arm clothed in glittering white which caught the sword and brandished it three times. And the hand and the sword vanished beneath the waves, for it was the Lady of the Lake, who had given the sword to King Arthur.

Sir Bedivere came again to the king and told him what he had seen. Then said King Arthur, "Help me to the shore."

Sir Bedivere carried the king from the battlefield to the edge of the lake. And there, drawn up on the beach, he saw a little boat with three fair queens standing in it, all robed in black. "Now put me into the boat," said the king, and so he did softly. And they took King Arthur in their arms and laid him on a couch that was there, weeping all the while.

Then Sir Bedivere cried out, "Ah, my lord Arthur, what shall I say of you to Lancelot when he comes, for he loves you well, and what shall become of your people, left among our enemies without you?"

"Take comfort," said the king. "Fear nothing. Trust in yourselves and do the best that you may. For I will go to the vale of Avalon to heal my grievous wound. And if you never hear of me again, pray for my soul."

Then the boat moved out from the shore and Sir Bedivere lost sight of it in the darkness.

King Arthur came no more to Britain, but some tell how he lives in Avalon, the Happy Isle, far in the Western Sea where it is always summer. In Avalon, they say, the heroes live forever. And still his people wait for Arthur to come again with all his knights around him, the once and future king.

The Isles of the Happy

Bran was king of the Isle of the Mighty, that is to say, king of Britain in the ancient days of Wales. Manawyddan was Bran's brother, and Llyr, the sea god, was his father. (They were the Irish Manannan and Lir.) Once, as Bran sat in his fort, surrounded by all his warriors, a strange woman appeared in their midst. She had come by magic, the gates being closed against all mortals, and she sang of the

Other World from which she had come. In that mysterious place, sea and land were so mingled that chariots could speed across the water and coracles could skim over the plains of earth. It was a world of many islands. She named them, one by one, each more beautiful than the last.

I bring a branch of *Evin*'s apple-tree,
In shape alike to those you know:
Twigs of white silver are upon it,
Buds of crystal with blossoms.

There is a distant isle,
Around which sea-horses glisten:
A fair course against the white-swelling surge—
Four pedestals uphold it.

A delight of the eyes, a glorious range
Is the plain on which the hosts hold games:
Coracle contends against chariot
In *Silver-white Plain* to the south.

Pedestals of white bronze underneath
Glittering through ages of beauty:
Fairest land throughout the world,
On which the many blossoms drop.

Then if *Silverland* is seen,
On which dragon-stones and crystals drop—
The sea washes the wave against the land,
A crystal spray drops from its mane.

Golden chariots on the plain of the sea
Heaving with the tide to the sun:
Chariots of silver on the *Plain of Sports*,
And of bronze that has no blemish.

If one has heard the voice of the music,
The chorus of little birds from the Land of Peace,
A band of women comes from a height
To the plain of sport in which he is.

There comes happiness with health
To the land against which laughter peals:
Into the Land of Peace at every season
Comes everlasting joy.

There are thrice fifty distant isles
In the ocean to the west of us:
Larger than Erin twice
Is each of them, or thrice.

Bibliography

Among the many sources which I have used in making this collection of Celtic myths, the following have been the most important and useful to me:

Ashe, Geoffrey, ed.: *The Quest for Arthur's Britain*. New York: Praeger, 1968.

Bulfinch, Thomas: *The Age of Chivalry*. Boston: Tilton, rev. ed., 1884.

Campbell, John F.: *Popular Tales of the West Highlands*. Edinburgh: Edmondston and Douglas, 1860.

Curtin, Jeremiah: *Myths and Folk-Lore of Ireland*. Boston: Little Brown, 1890.

Dillon, Myles: *Early Irish Literature*. Chicago: University of Chicago, 1948.

Dillon, Myles, and Nora Chadwick: *The Celtic Realms*. London: Weidenfeld & Nicolson, 1967.

Ebbutt, M. I.: *Hero-Myths and Legends of the British Race*. London: Harrap, 1910.

Geoffrey of Monmouth: *History of the Kings of Britain*. London: Dent, 1912.

Gregory, Lady Augusta: *Gods and Fighting Men*. London: John Murray, 1913.

Henry, Patrick Leo: *Early English and Celtic Lyric*. New York: Barnes & Noble, 1967.

Hull, Eleanor: *Cuchulain: The Hound of Ulster*. London: Harrap, 1909.

Jackson, Kenneth: *A Celtic Miscellany*. London: Routledge & Kegan Paul [1951].

Jacobs, Joseph: *More Celtic Fairy Tales*. London: Nutt, 1894.

Mabinogion, translated by Gwyn and Thomas Jones. New York: Dutton, 1949.

MacCana, Proinsias: *Celtic Mythology*. Feltham: Hamlyn, 1970.

Malory, Sir Thomas: *Le Morte D'Arthur*. The Text of Caxton ed. by Sir Edward Strachey. London: Macmillan, 1909.

Meyer, Kuno: *Selections from Ancient Irish Poetry*. London: Constable, 1911.

O'Grady, Standish Hayes: *Silva Gadelica*. London: Williams and Norgate, 1892.

O'Rahilly, R. F.: *Early Irish History and Mythology*. Dublin: Dublin Institute for Advanced Study, 1946.

Rees, Alwyn D.: *Celtic Heritage*. New York: Grove [1961].

Rolleston, Thomas W.: *The High Deeds of Finn*. New York: Crowell, 1910.

———: *Myths & Legends of the Celtic Race*. London: Harrap, [1911].

Scott, Sir Walter: *Minstrelsy of the Scottish Border*, ed. by Thomas F. Henderson. New York: Scribners, 1902.

Sjoestedt-Jonval, Marie Louise: *Gods and Heroes of the Celts,* translated by Myles Dillon. London: Methuen [1949].

Souvestre, Émile: *Le Foyer Breton.* Paris: Nelson [1925].

Yeats, William Butler, ed.: *Folk Stories and Fairy Tales.* New York: Random House, n.d.

Young, Ella: *Celtic Wonder Tales.* New York: Dutton, 1923.

———: *The Tangle-Coated Horse.* New York: McKay, 1929 and 1968.